What Others Are Saying About This Book

"Ken Yabuki engages the subject of human suffering in a way that is both lively and elegant. Every chapter is highly useful and insightful. He argues that suffering and adversity can actually strengthen one's Christian faith. He offers a practical and realistic approach to managing the dark times Christians go through."

Anthony So, Ph.D., D.Min.
Associate Professor of Practical Theology
Logos Evangelical Seminary

"Mr. Yabuki has conducted *listening seminars* at our annual conference in Japan for three years in a row. He has also had personal interactions with those struggling with emotional pains and many people, including myself, have been comforted. I have found this book very relevant for Japanese Christians because: 1) It is written by a 'wounded healer' who identifies himself with those who are going through suffering; 2) It deals with the problem of suffering from a Biblical perspective with a focus on the grace of God; and 3) It is a book that summarizes what the author has been practicing for over 50 years. I would like this book translated into Japanese. The Lord will bless many Japanese through this book."

Rev. Kenichi Nakagawa
President
Harvest Time Ministries, Japan

"Ken Yabuki addresses ultimate issues of life in a way that people can understand and relate to. He combines a biblically based pastoral perspective with his experiences as a therapist to help those going through pain and suffering. He not only presents rational arguments but also supports them with practical insights. This makes this book unique and helpful. As a hospital chaplain, I would recommend this book to my patients."

Davy Lin, M.Div., MFT
Hospital Chaplain, Los Angeles, CA

"Ken Yabuki offers a thoughtful and biblical perspective on the problem of pain and the hope found in Christ. What may surprise us, though it shouldn't, is that the power of Christ powerfully flows through us not primarily through our pontifications or pronouncements – however true these may be. Christ's love and truth overflows from Christians as they offer the gift of *listening.* I have personally experienced this ministry from him along with hundreds of others who have benefited through his ministry in the US and Japan. I trust the readers will benefit from his years of experience compiled in this succinct and yet thorough work."

Rev. Tim Yee
Senior Pastor
Union Church of Los Angeles

"Pastor Ken Yabuki brings his pastoral and counseling experiences together in a book to help believers understand and respond to the eternal questions about human suffering and the resulting emotional and spiritual challenges. Using the truth of Scripture and the tool of psychological counseling, he provides practical applications of what he has learned from his own research for truth via his experiences in the church and his years of working with clients as a therapist. He presents a well-researched, accessible book effectively communicating the pragmatic value of embracing God's grace. As a bilingual and bicultural individual, he provides examples and illustrations which will resonate with a variety of readers. A valuable resource for anyone of faith, personally struggling or assisting others with the difficult questions which arise from our human condition."

Alan Oda, Ph.D.
Professor of Psychology, Azusa Pacific University
Chairman, Board of Directors
Asian American Christian Counseling Service

Why Bad Things Happen To Good People

And What Can Be Done about It

A Christian Perspective

KEN YABUKI, M.DIV., MFT

Unless otherwise noted, all scripture verses quoted in part or whole are from the 1990 *New International Version* (NIV) of the Bible, published by Zondervan. Verses designated as NKJV are quoted from *The New King James Version*, published by Thomas Nelson Publishers, 1985. One hundred of the self-rating statements used by Dr. Raymond Cramer in his book *The Psychology of Jesus and Mental Health* are reproduced by permission of Zondervan.

WestBow Press books may be ordered through booksellers or by contacting:

WestBow Press
A Division of Thomas Nelson & Zondervan
1663 Liberty Drive
Bloomington, IN 47403
www.westbowpress.com
1 (866) 928-1240

ISBN: 978-1-4908-7695-5 (sc)
ISBN: 978-1-4908-7696-2 (hc)
ISBN: 978-1-4908-7694-8 (e)

Library of Congress Control Number: 2015905999

Print information available on the last page.

WestBow Press rev. date: 4/24/2015

Dedication

This book is dedicated to my wife Georgia who has been the love of my life for 45 years and to my son Preston and his family, Kathy, Nicholas and Jacob who bring so much joy and delight into my life.

Contents

Introduction ix

Chapter One: Different Perspectives On Why Bad Things Happen To Good People 1

Non-Christian Perspectives 1
Christian Perspectives 3

Chapter Two: Dealing With The Pain Of Suffering – A Christian Approach 9

Being Strengthened by the Word of God 9
Crying Out to God in Prayer When in Distress 16
Learning to Commune with God in Silence 16
The Lord is Only a Prayer Away 19
Christian Fellowship and the Ministry of Listening 20

Chapter Three: Growing Through Emotional Pain 30

Continued Quest for the "Why of Life" 30
When Prayers are Not Answered 33
Worry and Anxiety 39

Discouragement and Depression 41
Frustration, Anger and Resentment 48
Relationship Difficulties 52
Challenges in Marriage 56
Challenges in Parenting 60
The Problem of Aging 64

Chapter Four: Continuing To Grow Through
Emotional And Spiritual Challenges 67

Struggling with Doubt 67
The Power of Surrender 70
Living One Day at a Time 75
A Mark of Spiritual Maturity 77
Benefits of Suffering 81
The Power of Humility 85
Agape Therapy: A Christian Way of Being in
this Broken World 87

Chapter Five: Summing Up 99

Summary and Conclusion 99
Measuring Your Own Progress 100

Epilogue: When All Else Fails 105
Appendix: Spiritual/Emotional Difficulty Inventory 111
Recommended Readings 119
About the Author 121

Introduction

We live in a world with no scarcity of bad news and many people live with a sense of subliminal foreboding. All of us are exposed to the possibility of something bad happening to us and we may fear it is not a matter of *if* but *when.* Deep down we want to believe that if we do our best to be good people, we should be spared of anything tragic happening to us. However, we all know that the reality is not that simple. We know that "bad things" do happen to good people and that they can happen to us as well. Throughout history people have asked the question, "Why do bad things happen to good people?" Every day in our lives when faced with a difficult personal crisis many of us ask, "Why me?"

Many thoughtful persons have proposed various answers. Philosophers, theologians, religious teachers and others have addressed this issue for centuries and many of their answers are very helpful but the case is not yet closed. People continue to ask the question wanting to know *the* answer. Despite the warning of King Solomon against writing of many books (Ecclesiastes 12: 12b) I have decided to try my hand in writing this book to suggest some answers that might help at least some people who are struggling.

I am approaching the topic as a Christian who struggled with this issue for over 50 years. I have grappled with it in my own life and discussed it with the people I have tried to help as a counselor. Much of what I have to say may not be anything new since it is based on Biblical teachings which are familiar to all of us. If there is anything new, it would be that the answer is not to be found by attempting to discover some new and brilliant ideas to dispel the conundrum once and for all. Rather the answer is to be found as we go through our life's journey with the Lord as our Shepherd in the company of a few trusted friends with whom we can share the pain and joy of life. It is a growth process that occurs as we apply the word of God, learn to deeply commune with the Lord and interact with a few friends who can become our *listening partners.*

I would like to acknowledge my indebtedness to all the people by whom I have been impacted, including numerous Christian writers, teachers, pastors, friends, colleagues and many of the people I have had the privilege of counseling. I learn so much from my counselees because very often I see myself reflected in them.

Chapter One

Different Perspectives On Why Bad Things Happen To Good People

Throughout human history man has grappled with the question of why bad things happen to good people and religious and cultural traditions have come up with various ideas and perspectives. I have placed them in two broad categories, Christian and non-Christian. This is not meant to be a divisive statement. It is done in order to point out the significant difference between the non-Christian and the Christian approaches. The former primarily relies on man's self-efforts to deal with the problem of human suffering whereas the latter heavily enlists help from God. It should be noted that even Christians are frequently influenced by non-Christian ideas in some ways without being aware of it.

Non-Christian Perspectives

Karma is an old Hindu concept based on the idea that we come back to live on earth repeatedly and when bad things happen to us, we are paying for the evil deeds we committed in former lives. As we pay for our misdeeds committed in former lives with our suffering in the present life, we will eventually be freed of all our debts.

Buddhism teaches that suffering is caused by human desires and cravings. By learning to give up cravings we can reduce suffering. Also by not dwelling on the past or focusing on the future we can be spared of unnecessary pain.

Natural religions are based on a belief in a variety of deities and teach that bad things happen when the deities are displeased with people. In order to make the misfortunes go away or prevent them from happening, people must please the deities by practicing certain rituals or appease the evil spirits by making prescribed sacrifices.

Belief in "bad luck" is difficult to be rid of. It is easy for us to fall for a superstitious belief that certain things bring misfortunes. In America people feel uncomfortable about the number thirteen. Some hotels do not have the thirteenth floor. Some people may refuse to plan anything on a Friday which falls on the thirteenth day of the month. In Japan some hospitals have no fourth floors because the number four is pronounced "shi" which is also how the word "death" is pronounced in Japanese. Many ethnic and cultural traditions have similar beliefs. People believe that by avoiding those unlucky entities they can avoid bringing misfortunes on themselves. Even well-educated and enlightened people may feel a tinge of nervousness if they go against some of those beliefs.

Stoicism is practiced by people who believe that we must face difficulties in life with quiet courage and determination. Stoicism was made popular by the ancient Greeks known as Stoics but the idea is not limited to ancient Greece. It is an idea often praised as a heroic and honorable way to deal with life's difficulties.

Humanism is a modern Western approach to life, which asserts that man is the center of the universe. According to this philosophy, God is not able to help us. We must do everything on our own. We must focus on man's self-efforts to deal with the difficulties in life.

There is one common thread that runs through all of the non-Christian perspectives. The common denominator is the idea that the solution lies in what man does. The focus is on man's self-effort to deal with the problem of suffering. Whether the problems are caused by natural forces or by supernatural entities, man must take the action to deal with the problem by his own efforts. In the sections that follow, I discuss the Christian perspectives which emphasize that: 1) we cannot adequately deal with the problem of suffering by ourselves without help from God, and 2) we can actually grow spiritually and emotionally through suffering by receiving help from the Lord. This is the main theme of this book.

Christian Perspectives

The Bible teaches that our God is a good God who loves us. He is also all-powerful. If so, why is there suffering in this world? Why does God allow suffering to come to Christians who are His children? The following are some of the answers that can be gleaned from the Bible.

Discipline

God, the Father, disciplines His children out of His love for them just as human fathers discipline their children out of their love for them (Hebrews 12:7-13). As we are disciplined, we are expected to learn to sin less. As we go through the Lord's discipline, we may develop spiritual maturity and may learn not to commit obvious blunders that would bring pain. However, we are not finished yet. Next comes the process of pruning.

Pruning

In John 15: 1-2, Jesus talks about how our heavenly Father *prunes* us just as a gardener prunes fruitful branches in order to make them even more fruitful. Spiritual pruning can be more painful than discipline. When we are disciplined, we usually know we need and deserve it. But when we are pruned, we feel it is not fair. But this is a necessary step for us to go through if we are going to become more like Christ. Pruning frequently occurs when we are sinned against by someone else. We suffer as a result of someone else's sin. We feel we are innocent. We cry foul and say it is not fair. And we inadvertently end up sinning (missing the mark) in our response to the sins committed by others. We need to grow in our ability to deal with the sins of others by learning from the way Jesus dealt with it and grow to become more like Christ.

Sharing in the Suffering of Christ

As Christians we are called not only to believe in Christ, but also to suffer for Him (Philippians 1:29). We will experience various types of persecution for being a Christian if we remain faithful to Him (Philippians 3:10). Throughout history followers of Jesus Christ have encountered persecutions, ranging from mild to very severe. Even in the 21st century, many Christians suffer severe persecutions, including martyrdom, in various parts of the world. Those of us living in democratic societies experience limited degrees of persecution but there is no way we can escape from the *offence of the cross* when we remain faithful witnesses for Jesus Christ. However, we must be careful not to add to it through our own offensive attitudes or by being thoughtless or immature.

Divine Mysteries

The concepts of discipline, pruning and the offence of the cross may not be too difficult to understand. Those concepts can help explain how painful human experiences can be used by God to shape and mold us into His image. However, there are extreme tragedies that occur in life that defy human explanations. They are total mysteries which completely baffle our mind. Mysteries are experiences that defy logical explanations. With advancement in scientific knowledge, many things that were considered mysteries in the past are now being explained. However, there are things that happen in life that make no logical sense at all. For example, I do not know why millions of innocent Jewish people had to die in the Holocaust. I do not know why thousands of good and innocent people lose their lives in natural disasters. We often wonder why a young promising person is suddenly snatched away from us in a tragic accident or following a mysterious and fatal illness. We could cite hundreds of similar stories of a tragic nature that challenge and mystify our mind. Those events and experiences cannot be explained away as providing opportunities for discipline or pruning. They are far too extreme. There are also mysteries in the Bible that are difficult to explain. In the story of Job, God allowed Satan to inflict suffering on Job. Why does God allow Satan to make people suffer? Why doesn't God stop it? Those are some of the Biblical mysteries that are difficult for the human mind to comprehend.

However, the problem is not the mysterious event itself. The problem stems from the limitations of the human mind. There are no mysteries to God. As Creator of the universe, God knows all things. The problem is that the human mind is not able to comprehend all of the mysteries of the universe. The human mind heavily relies on the use of human logic. Human logic is far too narrow to comprehend all of the mysteries of God. We did not create this amazing universe, nor did we create ourselves. We are not all knowing. Only God is. The Lord told Isaiah, "As the heavens are higher than the earth, so are my ways higher than your ways and my thoughts than your thoughts" (Isaiah 55:9 NIV). For years I tried to understand Albert Einstein's theory of relativity and I still do not understand it completely. It seems that my mind is not capable of understanding Dr. Einstein's mind. If I cannot understand even the mind of Dr. Einstein, how can I expect to understand the mind of God?

When I was young, there was a time when I was under the illusion I knew everything. But the older I get, the more I realize how little I know about the mysteries of the universe and the mysteries of God. Man's biggest problem is himself. He wants to know everything. He wants to be in charge of the universe. But it is unrealistic for man to expect to be in charge of the universe. Only by accepting the reality of certain human limitations, we can have peace and contentment. The universe can take care of itself without us controlling it. Still some people refuse to accept their human limitations. I believe man has the ability to understand more and more of the physical mysteries of the universe and even to control it to some extent. But when it comes to metaphysical questions, the humility to admit our intellectual limitations would do more good for humanity than the prideful attitude which keeps on insisting that someday we will be as wise as God to understand all the mysteries of the universe. We rely on human logic to try to understand the mysteries of God but human logic is not adequate enough to understand divine mysteries. We can only deal with divine mysteries by faith but the human mind is not satisfied with it and the quest continues. (Additional discussions follow in Chapter Three under "Continued Quest for the 'Why of Life.'")

The Purpose of Suffering and the Promise of Redemption

The Bible teaches that the Lord uses suffering to accomplish certain purposes and in this sense no suffering is a wasted experience. Even though bad things can happen to any of us, we can be assured that "all things work together for good to them who love God and are called according to His purpose" (Romans 8:28 KJV). The problem, however, is that we cannot immediately see the "good" that can come out of the tragedy; it takes time for that to occur and sometimes we may never know in this life why certain things happen. In the meantime, we still experience pain but the pain can be made more bearable when we bring the pain to the Lord (Matthew 11:29). By following God's prescriptions, our yoke can be made easy and our burden light (Matthew 11:30).

Suffering is always accompanied by pain. And the Bible provides us with ways to help us deal with the pain of suffering. Unlike the non-Christian approaches which rely exclusively on self-efforts, the Bible teaches that we can come to the Lord and learn to rely on Him. When we are able to rely on God, it is amazing how much strength we can receive (II Corinthians 12:7-10). However, it is not magic. The pain will still be there. How can we deal with the mental and emotional pain that is part and parcel of this human experience?

Chapter Two

Dealing With The Pain Of Suffering – A Christian Approach

I have discovered there are three things that help accomplish God's purpose in our suffering; the word of God, prayer and authentic Christian fellowship. Those phrases are well-worn clichés that come from familiar Christian lingo. Many people simply pass over them without realizing the rich and deep spiritual treasures contained in them.

Being Strengthened by the Word of God

Emotional pain comes from the discrepancy between expectation and reality and the wider the gap between the two, the greater the pain. Reality is not always under our control but expectation is. We need to learn to formulate our expectations according to thinking based on the word of God. Therefore, reading and meditating on the word of God is of utmost importance if we are going to understand the mind of God.

The Bible is a book of reality that deals with the problem of pain and suffering. Contrary to the popular notion that the Bible is a neat, clean and respectable "G-rated" book, it actually depicts some of the most horrible and ugliest of human experiences. We need to train our mind to think realistically by reading the word of God. When we train our mind to think realistically by reading and meditating on the word of God, nothing that happens in this world should surprise us.

But the word of God does not leave us cynical and hopeless. It gives us a new direction to deal with reality. It gives us a new direction and hope in the person of Jesus Christ. The Bible can lead us to enter into a personal relationship with God in the person of Jesus Christ who is *God Incarnate*. God whom we cannot see became visible and touchable as a human being in the person of Jesus of Nazareth so that we may discover what God is like. Jesus said, "Anyone who has seen me has seen the Father" (John 14:9 NIV). Jesus of Nazareth personified the character of God.

By reading the word of God and with the help of the Holy Spirit we can enter into a personal relationship with God through Jesus Christ. And we can go through the rest of our life's journey with Him as our Guide here on earth and into eternity. This can provide a new meaning, purpose and direction for life. There are many Scriptures which touch on the meaning and purpose of suffering. They come alive when we discover how relevant they are as we go through life's journey which is punctuated with adversities. I would like to share some of those Scripture verses and passages that I have found to be helpful in my life.

The Scripture verses I have relied on most frequently whenever I am faced with a personal crisis are found in Proverbs Chapter 3 where it says, "Trust in the lord with all your heart and lean not on your own understanding; in all your ways acknowledge him and he will make your paths straight" (Proverbs 3:5-6 NIV). When I am faced with a problem, my first reaction is to try to change it. If I can change it, the problem goes away. When the problem does not go away, I try a little harder. If the problem is still not resolved, I try different strategies. If the problem persists after I have exhausted all of my options, I become frustrated. If I can remember Proverbs 3:5-6, I can acknowledge my need for the Lord's wisdom and help. When I recite those verses quietly in my mind, I become calmer and I can think more clearly, which helps me to address the issue at hand more effectively. If I can remember my need for the Lord's help sooner, I can cut short my initial frustration period and spare myself some of the agony. It takes practice to learn to call on the Lord sooner. Human nature being what it is, it is natural for us to struggle in our own strength until we get exhausted. There is always room for improvement for us to learn to shorten the time before we remember to call on the Lord.

It has been said that there are no atheists in fox holes. It seems to be our nature to cry out for God's help when we are in trouble. But when the trouble is over, it is easy to forget God and we go on our own merry way. Would it be possible that God allows hardships to come our way so that we will remember to come to Him? In II Corinthians 1:8-10, the Apostle Paul talks about the tremendous hardships he and his companions suffered when they were in the province of Asia. In fact, the pressures were so great that they were beyond their ability to endure and Paul and his companions despaired even of life, which meant that they were even feeling slightly suicidal or at least yearned for heaven (Philippians 1:23-24). We have a tendency to romanticize our Biblical heroes so as to think that people such as the Apostle Paul would be above experiencing suicidal thoughts. But such was not the case. Paul was just as human as anyone else. But the Apostle Paul made an important observation that the reason God allowed such painful hardships was so that he might not rely on himself but on God.

But what does it mean to rely on God? What happens when we learn to rely on God? In II Corinthians 12: 7-10 Paul describes what happened to him when he found himself to be totally helpless. He encountered a very painful problem which he described as *a thorn in his flesh.* No one knows exactly what the problem was because Paul does not tell us. But whatever it was, it was so painful that he pleaded with the Lord that it might be removed from him. One could not think of a more legitimate prayer request but the Lord said "No" to Paul. Instead of granting Paul's request, the Lord said to him, "My grace is sufficient for you, for my power is made perfect in weakness" (NIV). We do not know how long or how much Paul struggled with the answer he received from the Lord before he was able to accept it and say, "Therefore I will boast all the more gladly about my weaknesses so that Christ's power may rest on me." Then he went on to add, "That is why, for Christ's sake, I delight in weaknesses, in insults, in hardships, in persecutions, in difficulties. For when I am weak, then I am strong" (NIV). What a revelation!

I believe God is trying to show us through the experience of Paul that the grace of God is sufficient to sustain us in any circumstances that we may encounter and that we can truly experience the power of God only when we become totally weak and helpless, unable to help ourselves. Only when we "hit bottom" with nothing we can do in our own strength, we can truly experience the power of the resurrection.

Most of us may not go through as much suffering as the Apostle Paul did but it is comforting to know that such power is available when we become totally helpless. This power is made available when we totally surrender ourselves to the will of our heavenly Father. To me the most powerful prayer in the Bible is the prayer of Jesus in the garden of Gethsemane. When he was confronted with the prospect of the impending crucifixion, I believe the emotional pain experienced by Jesus was more excruciating than the physical pain of the crucifixion itself. Luke, the physician, reports that Jesus perspired blood in agony when anticipating the impending crucifixion. He was able to endure this excruciating emotional pain and work through the agony by interacting with his Father. He was heard to utter, "Father, if you are willing, take this cup from me; yet not my will, but yours be done" (Luke 22:42 NIV). Some people speculate that it must have taken Jesus a considerable amount of time for him to go from "Father, if you are willing, take this cup from me" to "yet not my will, but yours be done." Even though Jesus was the Son of God, he was one-hundred percent human and felt all of the human emotions that any of us would feel under those circumstances (Hebrews 5:8). It should be noted that when Jesus was able to pray that he was willing to surrender his destiny to the will of his Father, he regained his composure and returned to rejoin his disciples (Luke 22:45-46). Surrendering to the will of our heavenly Father who is infinitely wise is the key to victory.

The Bible shows that suffering accomplishes certain goals in our lives. In Romans 5:3-5 the Apostle Paul talks about how suffering produces perseverance; perseverance, character; and character, hope. Paul goes on to say that "hope does not disappoint us because God has poured out His love into our hearts by the Holy Spirit whom He has given us" (NIV). In James 1:2-4, the Apostle James reminds us that "the testing of our faith develops perseverance" but "perseverance must finish its work so that we may be mature and complete, not lacking anything (NIV)."

According to Paul and James, it is God's design to use suffering to build character in us by teaching us to persevere. Intuitively we can understand that long and sometimes painful training is required for us to accomplish anything worthwhile, whether in sports, academics, the arts or in the professions. Christians and non-Christians alike, all of us need to go through the same rigorous process to achieve anything worthwhile in life. The difference between the Christian approach and the non-Christian approach is whether or not one relies on God in the process. Those who make it without help from God will be proud of their accomplishments but they may also look down on those who do not make it. On the other hand, those who rely on God to accomplish great things will be humble, knowing that they were able to do it only with God's help. They will also be merciful toward those who are struggling and would be willing to offer help as a servant of God.

When character is developed in us, we can learn to hope without disappointment. Hope can be easily dashed unless it has been made deeply resilient by continuous character building. But this is not accomplished by our teeth-gritting efforts. It can only be achieved by experiencing the love and grace of God every step of the way with the help of the Holy Spirit who dwells in us. We can learn to surrender our fear and disappointment to the Lord as we continue to move ahead toward reaching our goals with hope. When we believe that our desires are given by the Lord (Philippians 2:13), we will be able to persistently pursue them as long as it takes or until the Lord redirects us. It should be noted that some of the things we hope for may not be achieved in our lifetime (Hebrews 11:13, 11:39-40) but if they are from the Lord they will eventually be fulfilled in the way designed by the Lord. What we need to do is to remain faithful to the leading of the Holy Spirit.

Many other verses and passages can be cited which touch on similar topics. I would encourage you, the reader, to identify those Scriptures that might apply to your own situations. It would be helpful to memorize those verses and meditate on them regularly. It would be helpful to discuss those Scriptures in Bible studies, hear them expounded in sermons or read about them in books. However, it is recommended that we refrain from quoting those Scriptures directly to a person who is in the midst of going through a very painful experience. Such persons are not ready to receive such information until their pain has at least somewhat subsided.

Job's "friends" made the mistake of doing this with Job. When Job, a righteous man, lost everything he had in his life, including his children, property and health for no fault of his own, he became very upset and angry with God. Job's three pious friends came to visit him and tried to help him by saying many things that were true. For example, Eliphaz, one of his friends, tells Job who was in the throes of agony, "Blessed is the man whom God corrects; so do not despise the discipline of the Almighty. For he wounds, but he also binds up; he injures but his hands also heal" (Job 5:17-18 NIV). Eliphaz shared those words of truth with Job with the intention of encouraging Job but Job was in no mood to receive such words of exhortation because his pain was so great. But his friends lacked the sensitivity to discern the emotional state Job was in and kept on preaching until Job could no longer take it and blurted out, "I have heard many things like these; miserable comforters are you all" (Job 16:2 NIV). Because of our own discomfort it is very tempting to lecture to a hurting person hoping to fix the person's problem to make it go away.

However, when the recipient of our intended encouragement is in the throes of emotional pain such words will fall on deaf ears.

For the words of God to deeply impact us, it is important that we read and meditate on them on a regular basis and to apply them in our daily experiences (Psalm 1:2-3) so that it will become second nature to us. But even then we will not be completely spared of pain.

Crying Out to God in Prayer When in Distress

When we are hurting we can honestly express our pain to the Lord. Our heavenly Father will not be surprised or offended when we pour out our deep and honest feelings to Him. The Book of Psalms is filled with painful cries and prayers of God's people who are deeply and desperately hurting. After we express our deepest hurts and feelings to the Lord, it will be helpful to wait quietly on the Lord in silence so that we may be able to hear Him speak to us in "a still small voice" (I Kings 19:11-12). It is vital that we commune with the Lord regularly. Jesus regularly withdrew to a quiet place to commune alone with his Father (Luke 5:16).

Learning to Commune with God in Silence

"Be still and know that I am God", we read in Psalm 46:10. I have found silence to be a helpful way to commune with the Lord. In my early years as a Christian I used to attend weekly prayer meetings at the church as expected of all good Christians. People would gather and ask for prayers and we would take turns praying. Most of the prayer requests were related to people's needs for healing, protection, guidance, etc. Some were labeled as "unspoken requests." After a while we would run out of things to pray for and the meeting would come to an end. I accepted those prayer meetings as part of my Christian duties.

About twenty years ago our church decided to have a prayer meeting in the sanctuary at seven AM on Sunday mornings. A group of people came together and prayed in the usual manner. After a few weeks the number of people coming to the meeting began to dwindle until there were only two or three people left. I thought about dropping out but something kept me from doing so. I would come every Sunday and just sit in the sanctuary by myself alone or with one or two other persons. By now we all prayed in silence. I sat in the middle of the sanctuary in silence. It was a strange experience. It was even unnerving at first. I felt uncomfortable. My mind would wander from one thing to another. Once in a while I would bring myself back to focus on Jesus and then my mind would drift off again.

It was a strange experience at first but as time went on it became more natural. I was learning to sit in total silence with intermittent awareness of God's presence. I continued the practice for a year or two (I do not recall exactly how long) until the time came when I was no longer able to arrive at the church at seven in the morning due to a change in my residential location away from the church by a considerable distance. But what I learned was to sit quietly in the presence of the Lord.

Now I make it my practice to spend time alone in silence whenever I can. I have a busy counseling schedule. I drive from my day time office to my evening office which are in two different locations. Before I get to my evening office,

I park my car on a quiet street to sit in silence and to spend time with the Lord. I am learning to experience the grace of God by doing absolutely nothing. Frequently I find myself dozing off. Sometimes I am not sure if I am awake or asleep. But when I finish my quiet time, I am rejuvenated. Troubling thoughts about some of my day time clients are all but gone and I am ready to work with my evening clients. During my quiet time with the Lord some of the painful memories of the past resurface. As I unhurriedly revisit the painful thoughts and emotions of those past experiences, I receive healing with new insight. The memories that are brought back may come from my childhood or from a more recent past; it could even be a painful emotion I experienced earlier in the day. It is during those quiet times with the Lord that I receive insight which brings healing and closure on some of my painful memories which negatively affect my thinking and behavior.

Those protracted quiet times with the Lord can be very peaceful or they can be deeply agonizing, depending on what I am going through at the time. When I happen to be going through a particularly challenging time, the quiet time with the Lord becomes a spiritual workshop in which I learn to surrender to Him the last vestige of my doubt about His will and plan for my life. During those times I need to become completely still so that I can hear Him speak to me *in a still small voice*. During those times the Lord may bring to my memory certain relevant words of Scripture. He may also remind me of His plan for my life from the very beginning till now and beyond. I vacillate back and forth between faith and doubt until I go deep in my silence and continue to interact with Him as He quietly impresses on my heart His plan. When I finally agree with Him and cease from vacillation, I experience *the peace of God which passes all understanding* and feel the joy of the Lord in my heart.

When the silent prayer session is over, I feel the warmth of His love in my heart with the reminder that I have a place to go to in times of my desperate spiritual need. I come away with the knowledge that I can always count on finding the Lord when I go deep in silence. Depending on the issues at hand, I may need a single or multiple silent prayer sessions with the Lord until I find resolution with a new direction. When faced with a spiritual or emotional crisis, it is useful (and recommended) to seek help from counselors or spiritual mentors but in the end there is none like the Wonderful Counselor who knows us better and loves us more than anyone else in the world. There are certain issues in life which are so personal and deep that only the Wonderful Counselor can help us deal with them. It has been my experience that we can meet with this Wonderful Counselor by going through protracted periods of deep silence and meditation.

The Lord is Only a Prayer Away

I have learned that the Lord is indeed a very present help in times of trouble (Psalm 46:1). Whenever I am faced with a challenge in my life, I have learned to send a quick SOS call to the Lord. "Lord, I need your help" has become my most frequently uttered prayer in recent years. Some people might call it "a breath prayer." Whenever I can remember to pray this split-second prayer, things somehow seem to work out better. When I fail to pray, I struggle until I catch myself and then remember to pray. I noticed that when I pray, the turbulence in my heart gives way to calmness and I can think more clearly. When the problem is resolved or at least becomes manageable, I thank the Lord for helping me, which doubles my joy. I am beginning to wonder if the Lord allows, or even brings, certain challenges to come my way so that I will have an opportunity to reach out to Him. Otherwise, I may stay away from the Lord for long periods of time due to my human tendency to forget the Lord.

It would be much better, of course, if I can remember the Lord continually throughout my waking hours regardless of whether or not I am being challenged with a problem. A long time ago a friend of mine suggested that I try to remember the Lord every fifteen minutes. I thought this was an interesting idea. I decided to give it a try. After many years of trying, I am yet to succeed in it. But I have also noticed that I do not let too many hours go by without remembering the Lord. Brother Lawrence mastered the art of *practicing the presence of Christ* wherever he was. He learned to stay continuously in the presence of the Lord while he worked in the busy kitchen of the monastery. It is reported that eventually he found little difference between the time he spent working in the kitchen and the time he spent on his knees praying.

Christian Fellowship and the Ministry of Listening

When we talk to the Lord in prayer, we believe He hears us but we cannot see Him. God is invisible but we can become God's *ears* which are visible. In Christian fellowship the Lord can use us to listen to one another as His visible representatives by becoming His ears. In the Christian community, we are familiar with the phrase the *ministry of speaking* but there is also a need for the *ministry of listening.* Large congregations usually have small group ministries where small groups of people come together to form more intimate relationships with one another. This is where listening becomes very important. The level of human interaction is determined by how we listen. An interaction between two individuals can be superficial or deep, depending on how we listen. Many people yearn for meaningful relationships. But we cannot have a meaningful relationship with another person unless we learn to listen well. How can we improve our listening skills? There are many effective listening techniques that are recommended by counselors. They are usually called *active listening techniques* and they can help us become better listeners. Over the past few years I have become acquainted with a listening technique called OARS, developed by Motivational Interviewing (MI) practitioners, which has wide application possibilities for use in Christian ministry (1). I have found this to be a very helpful listening tool. I use it in my counseling practice and I also teach it in my listening workshops.

OARS is an acronym for *O*pen-ended questions, *A*ffirm, *R*eflect and *S*ummarize. When OARS is effectively used, relationships between individuals can become deep and meaningful. I conduct listening workshop for Christian groups, in which I introduce the participants to simple yet effective listening techniques based on OARS. In my listening workshops each participant is paired up with a partner of the same gender and of similar age. The partners are instructed to take turns talking and listening to one another. The subject of conversation could be some painful topic or a more neutral one. The listener begins by asking an open-ended question, such as "What has been the most painful experience in your life?" or "What made you decide to come to the workshop today?" Whatever the answer is, the listener's job is to *affirm* what was said. We can usually do this by repeating what we think we heard. We can also do this by *rephrasing* what we think we heard. Once we decide the answer was understood correctly, we might offer a brief *summary* of what we think we heard. We can repeat this process by continuing to ask additional open-ended questions and offering affirmation until our partner feels adequately understood. When one partner is finished, it is time to switch roles to allow the other partner to repeat the same process. Not everyone is endowed with a natural gift for listening but the ability to listen can be learned and developed with practice with the use of a listening tool such as OARS.

Ever since I learned to incorporate OARS in my counseling practice, I have been finding counseling to be less stressful and more enjoyable. It is as if I am floating down the stream in a boat with another person using a pair of oars to guide the journey. There is little struggle involved with no direct confrontation. When the conversation takes a negative turn, I can gently bring it back by asking open-ended questions. When a negative statement comes up, I can gently redirect it by asking questions touching on the emotions behind the negative statement, such as "I wonder what makes you feel that way?" When negative answers are given I continue to affirm them until the person is relieved of the negative emotions which gave rise to the initial negative statement. When the person is set free, even in a small measure, from the negative emotions, he/she can begin to be more rational.

When negative emotions are aroused by negative thoughts or memories, the part of the brain known as the *emotional center* is activated, which overrides the part of the brain that engages in logical thinking. By using the OARS technique we are able to gradually defuse the activated emotional center of the brain to allow the *logical thinking center* of the brain to be re-activated. When the brain's logical thinking capability is restored, we are able to engage in a more meaningful conversation. There are at least two positive outcomes I have noted since I started using the OARS listening technique. One is that I have seen some remarkable changes take place in some of the most difficult counselees I have worked with. The second is that I no longer experience burnout in my counseling practice. When I am able to adequately understand another human being, it is a gratifying and energizing experience.

If the OARS technique is too cumbersome to remember, there is a simpler way of listening that may be just as effective. Proverbs 17:28 says, "Even a fool is thought wise, if he keeps silent, and discerning if he holds his tongue" (NIV). Listening in silence without saying a word can be just as effective in some situations as using the OARS listening technique. I have experienced it in my counseling practice and I have heard other people talk about it as well.

The most memorable story I heard was told by an American missionary in Japan. This missionary was also a counselor. When he first arrived in Japan, he did not understand or speak any Japanese. But a pastor who had heard he was a counselor asked him to help a woman who was in some sort of distress. He hesitantly agreed and met with the woman who blurted out her problems to him in Japanese. The missionary just listened. When it was over he did not know if he had helped her or not. A few days later the missionary saw the pastor who excitedly told him, "I don't know what you did with her but she is fine now!"

In the story of Job in the Old Testament, the friends of Job were speechless when they first saw Job in his great agony. Job's suffering was so great that they did not know what to say. They just sat with Job for seven days and seven nights without saying a word (Job 2:13), which allowed Job to vent his frustration. This was evidently helpful to Job. But after a while his friends could no longer stand the pain Job was in and they began to lecture to Job. They thought they were helping Job by telling him the truth but it did more harm than good and made Job extremely distressed (Job 16:2).

All of us need someone to listen to us when we are in distress. I learned the value of listening accidentally (or providentially) when I was in my first year of seminary. I became a Christian in Japan during my freshman year in college. I became very excited about my Christian faith and became somewhat of a campus evangelist. I would tell fellow students that they should become Christians because when one becomes a Christian all of life's problems can be resolved. I managed to maintain this naïve belief the rest of my college years. When I graduated from college, I felt called to go to seminary. In the fall of 1961, I arrived in Pasadena, California to begin studies at Fuller Theological Seminary. It was a new experience for me. Even though I did not have language problems because I had been an English major in college, I was not fully acclimated to the American culture. For the first time in my Christian life, I began to have problems I could not resolve. Still I maintained that I should be able to cope with my problems with my faith in Jesus Christ.

One day a fellow student who evidently sensed that I was distressed told me about a small group that met on Saturday mornings. It was a group meeting where students would come together to share their burdens and talk about their personal struggles with one another. I did not think I would be interested but somehow I found myself sitting in the back of the group the following Saturday morning. People were sharing their personal problems while others listened. I sat in the back of the room saying to myself, "I will never share my problems. Not me." A few days later I happened to be talking with a fellow student and suddenly we began to share our personal struggles with each other. We found it helpful so we decided to do it on a regular basis. Every night after the library closed, we would come together to share our burdens. One of us would talk and the other would listen. We took turns talking and listening. We found it to be so helpful that we continued the practice the rest of the academic year. Ever since that time I have made it my practice to always look for at least one person with whom I can mutually share my burdens. This has proved to be a very beneficial experience and it has given me the idea of engaging in the ministry of listening.

The relationship advocated in the ministry of listening is not like the professional relationship between a counselor and a counselee, in which the counselor is expected to be the expert with answers. The relationship to be developed in the ministry of listening is a mutual relationship between two individuals taking turns talking and listening to one another. I believe this is a very practical way to *bear one another's burdens* (Galatians 6:2). The important thing is not to give advice but to listen. It is the Holy Spirit who gives the right advice and direction. Our job is to listen. Of course it is recommended that we seek professional help when we have problems that we cannot resolve by ourselves even with the help of a good listener. But I also believe that for many of the ordinary problems we face in life, having a listening partner will be of significant help. And I believe the Christian community is a natural place for this to occur. Authentic Christian fellowship can be created among members of the Christian community when they can learn to listen to one another with humility and empathy. The ministry of listening can also be a helpful adjunct to professional counseling.

A word of caution is in order at this juncture. We must guard against the possibility of spreading gossip that could damage the relationship between the individuals involved. We must be very careful not to disclose what we hear to anyone else. If we believe in the *priesthood of all believers* it is appropriate that we minister to one another by listening. But we also have a sacred duty to safeguard sensitive information entrusted to us while engaging in the ministry of listening. If what we are hearing happens to be too disturbing, we might talk with our pastor or seek some professional help. We might decide to confide in our pastor or talk with a professional counselor but we must not confide in anyone else.

There is an area in which good listening is badly needed but not easily obtained. It is in a marital relationship or with close relatives whose wellbeing directly impacts us. It may not be difficult to listen to a person in distress if the person is a stranger but when it happens to be someone close to us, such as our spouse or another close member of the family, we would find it almost impossible to listen objectively. To be able to listen effectively to someone who is close to us, we need to change our mindset. We would need to switch from our usual way of thinking to a deeper one. Only when we can remember that the Lord is in control of our lives and that our destiny is in the Lord's hands, we would be able to listen calmly to a loved one. When we realize our loved ones are "on loan" to us from the Lord, we can minister to them effectively. It would be helpful to rehearse those possibilities mentally in our quiet time so that when a family crisis does occur we will be prepared. It would also be helpful to remember the words of the Apostle James who reminds us that life on earth is like a mist that could evaporate at any moment (James 4:14-15). But if we are unable, for whatever reason, to provide effective listening to a loved one who is in dire need of it, we should seek the assistance of a pastor or a professional counselor.

However, the most difficult challenge in listening does not usually come from crisis situations that occur in a family. Rather it is frequently encountered in marital relationships. There is a common complaint that comes from a husband (or sometimes a wife) who says, "I get so tired of listening to my spouse complain about the same thing over and over. Do you think she/he will ever get over it?" This is a dilemma experienced by spouses who try to be supportive to each other but get frustrated in the process. Some people try to deal with it by confronting their spouses and challenging them to "grow up." This approach may or may not work, depending on the emotional readiness of the spouse who is being challenged. When it does not work, which is usually the case, we need to go deeper. We would need to learn to listen to our spouse more deeply in order to understand the feelings behind the negativity. By following the OARS listening technique, we will be able to understand the negative feelings being experienced by our spouse. Behind the negative words are hidden emotions of anger and/or fear. In order to address those emotions, we can begin by asking an open-ended question, such as, "I wonder what makes you so upset (or frustrate)?" Whatever answer is given, we need to *affirm* it. When those emotions are affirmed, rather than criticized or analyzed, they can become less negative. When this occurs it will pave a way to a more rational interaction. The couple can then engage in a more meaningful conversation. It is not necessary to find an answer to the problem. When the deep and hidden emotions are acknowledged and accepted, the pain is reduced and the struggle becomes more manageable. When this pattern of interaction is established, even negative remarks can open a door to a deeper and more meaningful interchange. This is how a couple can minister to one another and grow together emotionally and spiritually. This type of interaction can deepen and strengthen the marital relationship. When we learn to listen to our spouse without judgment, our spouse can feel safe enough to bring up the most personal and sensitive issues which can be meaningfully worked through over time with the help of the Holy Spirit. For this to occur, however, the listener must be totally committed to the Lord and ask for His help continuously along the way.

The foregoing discussion describes an ideal scenario of how a couple can utilize the OARS listening technique to deepen their relationship with one another but in reality it can be much more challenging. Being able to affirm what is being said by our spouse is very difficult when the statement happens to be a negative one. Instead of being able to affirm the statement, we will automatically react with the "righting reflex" which is a term used by Motivational Interviewing practitioners to refer to our natural human tendency to correct the negative tone of a statement. For example, when a wife or a husband makes a statement such as, "I don't like our new pastor", a natural response will most likely be something like "You shouldn't feel that way." At this point the conversation will either stop or escalate into an argument and the couple will miss out on an opportunity to get to know each other more deeply. If the listener could respond by making a statement such as "I wonder why you feel that way", the conversation can go deeper and the couple can learn more about each other, including why the negative statement was made in the first place. For a couple to be able to go deeper, they must be willing to continue to engage in the ministry of listening with one another to improve their listening skills by learning from the mistakes they make. It requires commitment and willingness to learn from mistakes if a couple is going to learn the art of listening. It is an art that can be learned by continual practice. To understand one's spouse requires not only commitment to the relationship but also a commitment to learning more effective listening skills. When two people fall in love and get married, they usually do not lack commitment but their commitment gets challenged and weakened when they continue to argue and fight with one another. When the couple learns to use an effective listening skill, the struggle can be made easier. Couples who try hard to accept one another without an effective listening skill sometimes do so by resigning to a sense of cynicism. Husbands (and even some wives) are sometimes heard making bemoaning statements such as "If you want to be happy in your marriage, just say 'you are right, dear' and that will get you off the hook every time." By learning to use an effective listening skill we can achieve more complete understanding and deeper acceptance of our spouse. When this occurs the couple will experience a sense of excitement and victory in their marriage rather than settle for subtle fatalism with a sigh of resignation. (Additional discussion to follow under "Challenges in Marriage" in Chapter Three.)

Chapter Three

Growing Through Emotional Pain

Continued Quest for the "Why of Life"

Viktor Frankl survived the Nazi concentration camp by remembering the words of Friedrich Nietzsche who said, "When a man knows the why of life, he can endure almost any how." Dr. Frankl kept himself alive by looking for reasons to live each day of his imprisonment at Auschwitz. Wanting to know *why* can provide reasons for living. It generates a drive for continued search. Not knowing why is very unsettling and the mind continues to look for answers to fill the vacuum. When we do not know why bad things happen to good people, our mind goes after an answer. The answers we come up with may or may not be correct but the human mind demands an answer that can bring closure. For anyone raised with a Judeo-Christian worldview, the existence of a God who is loving and all powerful and yet allows bad things to happen presents a knotty problem. Rabbi Harold Kushner, the author of *When Bad Things Happen to Good People*, was able to reconcile this dilemma by concluding that God was unable to help with the illness of his son because God was helpless to do so. Those who adhere to a deistic view of God believe that the Creator God left this universe to let it run on its own devices. Carl Jung, the psychoanalyst, in his book *Answer to Job*, suggested that perhaps God should have apologized to Job for what he did. The human mind tries to relieve itself of the pressure from this problem by finding philosophical answers to bring closure. But the problem does not go away permanently and we continue to grapple with this problem that has no easy answers. And the search continues. There are many Christian writers who have written excellent and helpful books on the subject of suffering and some of those books, from which I have learned a great deal, are listed under "Recommended Readings." Those books have helped me to exercise my intellectual curiosity to the full; they have also directed me to search for practical answers from a pastoral counseling perspective.

In the story of Job who so desperately wanted to know the answer for his suffering, God never gave Job a direct answer. Instead, God spoke to Job through a storm (Job 38:1), which seemed to have shaken him out of his usual way of thinking. The fierce storm seemed to have jogged Job's mind in such a way that his mind was opened to new realities that he was unaware of before. I remember being in a storm with powerful downpours of rain, accompanied by fierce winds, as well as thunder and lightning. The strong winds broke tree branches which fell on the street below. A particularly large branch, as it fell, severed high voltage electric wires. The electric wires were now dangling in the street below filled with gushing rain water. The sparks ignited by the live electric wires which fell on the street were frightening and spectacular. As I was watching this amazing sight in awe from the second floor of my apartment, I completely forgot my usual challenges of life. It was a healing experience. I realized there was a world out there which was bigger than my own little world. It gave me a larger perspective on life and when I went back into my own world after the storm subsided, my daily life struggles seemed less ominous. I have had other similar experiences with some spectacular sights of nature which reminded me of the awesome mysteries of the universe and the Creator behind it. When Job realized the awesomeness of God, his mindset was changed and his struggles ceased. His perceptions changed and he was at peace again. He was restored to health and in the end he was blessed twice as much as before.

It seems to me that the problem is not what happens out there in the universe; it is the limitation of the human mind which is unable to understand the mysterious reality of life as we experience it. I do not believe this quest can be satisfied by intellectual pursuit alone. It can only be satisfied when we truly *worship God* in awe to have our mind stretched to recognize God for who He is. But we would never be able to understand God completely. If we did, He would not be God.

No matter how much we try to understand why bad things happen to good people, it is unlikely that we will be able to obtain an answer which will be universally acceptable. It has been said it is impossible for the finite human mind to fully understand God who is infinite. But man's curiosity will not rest until it finds an answer that satisfies it. So the pursuit continues. But when the object of the pursuit is related to *infinity* which by definition has no ending, the pursuit is likely to have no ending. But human curiosity will continue to drive us in this quest. Even though the quest may end up being a quest for the sake of quest itself, it is not to say that the pursuit is meaningless. I believe the quest is useful in that it meets the need of human curiosity which seeks closure. However, intellectual pursuit alone will most likely fall short of finding completely satisfactory closure.

I believe there is a more productive (and perhaps less agonizing) alternative. Instead of trying to answer the question of *why* regarding a problem that seemingly has no satisfactory answers, we can be asking *how* we could best deal with it when it occurs. C.S. Lewis observed that great suffering seems to provide opportunities for great heroism. History is replete with stories of people who have overcome great adversities to inspire the rest of us. Helen Keller is a classic example. Modern day heroes include Joni Eareckson-Tada, Bob Wieland and Nicholas Vujicic, to name a few. There are countless other heroes whose names are not well-known. Those heroes have inspired me to have a deeper look at my own life. Those heroes encourage all of us by providing much needed role models to emulate. Their examples can help us come out of our "pity parties" when we are frustrated with some inconveniences we encounter. Those individuals seem to have graduated from the initial stage of asking *why* to the next stage of deciding *what to do* about it. They are the pioneers, heroes and champions in the field of suffering. It is not to say that they no longer suffer but their suffering has a purpose and direction. They are no longer going around in circles, asking questions with no satisfactory answers. Instead they are now focused on creatively and courageously finding ways to accomplish the purpose of their "disability" in a new direction. Those individuals can truly inspire the rest of us and help us meet the challenges of life we all face.

When Prayers are Not Answered

When I was a young Christian in college, my reading assignments for English literature included such authors as W. Somerset Maugham and others, whose philosophies of life were not friendly toward the Christian faith. Somerset Maugham in his autobiographical novel *Of Human Bondage* poignantly portrays a very sensitive experience in the life of a young boy named Philip, which has a profound spiritual impact on Philip (actually on Maugham himself) and for anyone else who reads the story.

Philip is a young English boy with a slight physical handicap (a club foot), which makes it difficult for him to participate in physical activities at the school. He was orphaned at age ten and was placed under the care of his uncle who is a clergyman. He is sent off to a boarding school where he is exposed to a spiritual revival of sorts. He hears how God answers prayers and it occurs to him that if he asked God, his deformed foot might be healed. He decides to give it a try.

During the winter recess he comes home and every night he kneels down to pray on the hard wooden floor of his bedroom. The wooden floor is very cold in the middle of winter in England but he perseveres. A special day is coming at the school when all the children will be participating in an all-day athletic event. Philip has always dreamed of being able to play like the other children. Now he has hope that God will grant his wish. He prays that the day he goes back to school his foot will be made well.

The day finally arrives. Philip wakes up early in the morning. This is the day he has been waiting for. He trembles with excitement as he slowly reaches down to feel his deformed foot. Is it healed? Did God answer Philip's prayers? To his disappointment, his foot is still the same, deformed.

Philip goes downstairs for breakfast. His uncle comments that Philip is particularly quiet this morning, not realizing what has been transpiring. Philip concludes that God did not answer his prayer because he did not have enough faith. So he resolves to try again. But after a while, unable to continue to bear the burden of the tension between hope and doubt, he decides to give it up. It makes me shudder to think how many people might go through similar experiences and turn away from their Christian faith.

But not everyone gets disillusioned as Phillip did. I have known people, some among my own acquaintances, who found themselves in a situation not unlike that of Philip and were actually healed of their physical handicaps in a truly miraculous manner. In the late 1960's I worked with a pastor named Samuel Arai in Japan. He was a gifted evangelist. When I returned to the US, I lost contact with him. A while later I heard a rumor that Rev. Arai had become "charismatic." Some years ago I was invited to attend a Bible conference sponsored by one of our sister churches. (This was an "ethnic church" that reached out to the Japanese-speaking residents in the area.) There were several guest speakers at the conference, some of whom had come from Japan. The conference was conducted bilingually in English and Japanese and I was asked to be a translator for one of the pastors from Japan. The pastor, for whom I was to provide translation, was Rev. Kato. Before he gave his message, Rev. Kato asked if his wife could give her testimony. I had never met Mrs. Kato before and I was to provide translation for her. She began to tell her story.

Mrs. Kato was born prematurely. At birth she was totally deaf along with a somewhat disfigured face. As a child she had to undergo many reconstructive surgeries to make her look more normal. At one of those times when she was in the hospital to have plastic surgery, a missionary came by and gave her some literature that said God loved her. Mrs. Kato, a teenager then, thought to herself, "You've got be kidding! If Go loved me, why am I like this?" However, eventually she gave her life to Christ and she became a Christian.

When Mrs. Kato was in college, she learned of a Rev. Samuel Arai who conducted "healing services" at a summer camp. She decided to go to the camp, hoping to be healed of her deafness. Rev. Arai prayed for her at the camp but nothing happened. She went home disappointed, wondering why she was not healed. A few days later Mrs. Kato was standing in the kitchen when she heard the sound of water coming out of the faucet for the first time in her life. Today she can hear perfectly well. She is happily married with children. She has a beautiful singing voice and she sings duet with her husband.

Do miraculous healings occur today? Anecdotal accounts of healing through prayer abound. But are they scientifically verifiable? A pioneering study was conducted at San Francisco General Hospital in the late 1980's (2). The researchers divided the patients in the coronary care unit of the hospital into two groups. One was the experimental group and the other the control group. The two groups were matched with regards to age, gender, diagnoses and the severity of the symptoms. The names of the patients in the experimental group were sent to several prayer groups so that they could be prayed for. The patients who were being prayed for were not informed of it. The researchers involved in the project did not know which patients were being prayed for and which ones were not. The patients in both groups received the same level of medical care.

After a period of time the health indicators of the patients in the two groups were compared. The results showed that the patients who were prayed for did better than those who were not. The differences noted in the health indicators of the patients between the two groups could not be explained on the basis of chance, the medical treatment received or any other variable. The only logical explanation was that the prayers helped the patients in the experimental group, though the traditional medical community is still reluctant to admit such possibilities. When a patient is miraculously cured, the medical terminology for it is "spontaneous remission." However, times are changing and the medical community is slowly becoming more open to the idea that prayers do work in ways that are not logically understood.

Having stated my belief in the power of prayer for supernatural healing, however, I must also admit that I have known many people whose prayers were not answered as wished. I have also known individuals who were healed of their illnesses through prayer and rejoiced for a while but eventually succumbed to their illnesses and died. Jesus healed many from their diseases. Jesus even raised Lazarus from the dead. But all of them eventually died. What does this mean? I do not believe Jesus came to establish a new school of alternative medicine to heal through prayer to compete with the traditional medical establishment. According to the Bible, Jesus performed miracles in order to demonstrate that He was indeed the Son of God. We must guard against the temptation to treat miracles as any more or less than what they are meant to be. I believe miracles are used by God to demonstrate to us that He is God who is able to temporarily change the laws of nature which He established in order that some people may be helped to believe.

When miracles do not happen, some people attribute it to lack of faith. Others might say God is powerless to do anything about diseases and tragedies. I do not believe either is the case. Jesus said faith as small as a mustard seed could move mountains. If a miracle is going to happen, it will happen regardless of the size of our faith. I believe when miracles do not seemingly occur as we expect them, God has His own reasons which are not obvious to us at the time, or they may never become clear to us on this side of eternity. At any rate, when miracles do not occur as hoped, some people walk away from God but others go deeper.

The Apostle Paul suffered from a painful condition which he described as *the thorn in the flesh* (II Corinthians 12:7). Biblical scholars have not been able to determine exactly what he suffered from. Whatever it was, it was so painful to Paul that he repeatedly asked the Lord to remove it. But the Lord did not take it away. Instead, He said to Paul, "My grace is sufficient for you, for my power is made perfect in weakness" (II Corinthians 12:9a NIV). Rather than walk away in disappointment, Paul used this experience to go deeper in his faith and learned that he could become strong when he was weak (II Corinthians 12:8-10). Paul's secret was surrender. The willingness to surrender is the key to spiritual growth. It is the willingness to surrender to God's will, or the lack of it, that determines whether a disappointing experience will make or break a person. Maugham went away disappointed. Paul went deeper in his faith.

I have been disappointed many times by unanswered prayers, as well as encouraged by answered prayers. However, when I look back on my "unanswered prayers", I am glad that the Lord said "No" to those prayers. I can now see the Lord's wisdom in it. I am learning that I can truly trust in the Lord's wisdom and guidance. Proverbs 19:21 says, "Many are the plans in a man's heart, but it is the Lord's purpose that prevails" (NIV). I have taken this verse to heart and I am finding my walk with the Lord much more exciting. It is the Lord who opens and closes doors. I walk through every door He opens and when He closes a door I look around for another door to open. It gives me a sense of adventure; it also takes unnecessary frustration out of my life.

Worry and Anxiety

Everyone worries from time to time. But when worry turns into anxiety it can interfere with life. Some people tend to be more anxiety-prone than others. It may have something to do with our nervous system. Some people seem to have more sensitive nervous systems than others. Severe anxiety is a debilitating emotion. It can emotionally cripple a person. When plagued by recurring panic attacks or bouts of severe anxiety that interfere with our functioning, it is important to seek professional help. But when dealing with more or less normal anxieties, the Bible offers helpful remedies.

In his letter to the Philippians, the Apostle Paul said, "Do not be anxious about anything, but in everything, by prayer and petition, with thanksgiving, present your requests to God. And the peace of God, which transcends all understanding, will guard your hearts and minds in Christ Jesus" (Philippians 4:6-7 NIV). When we memorize those words and meditate on them regularly and put them into practice, we can be gradually changed and will no longer need to be enslaved by this gnawing emotion. First, we need to honestly admit to the Lord that we are anxious. The Lord knows our heart and He knows we are anxious. When we confess our anxiety to the Lord, He does not condemn us. He is glad that we opened up to Him about it. When we admit our anxiety, it may subside a little. Secondly, we are to give thanks. As long as we are in a complaining mood, we are "under the pile" but when we begin to give thanks, we can come out from under it. This further relieves the pressure. Thirdly, we need to search our heart and see what is causing the anxiety. When I am feeling anxious, I often find in my heart some hidden fear, from which I am trying to escape. It is an exaggerated fear of something I would not be able to handle if it should occur. I need to face this fear. What I need to do is to get to the bottom of the fear by asking myself what would be the worst possible case scenario. Then I ask myself if there is anything I could do about it in my power. If there is something I could do, I need to come up with a plan. But if not, I need to leave it in the Lord's hand and leave it there. Thus I can experience the *peace of God that transcends all understanding* and my heart is guarded from the ravages of runaway anxiety. When vague anxiety is made more specific, it becomes more manageable. For an anxiety-prone person, this process will need to be repeated over a long period of time before freedom from anxiety can be achieved to become a lasting reality.

I have always known myself to be an anxious person. Anxiety proneness has some advantages. For example, I seldom miss deadlines because I am a conscientious planner. But it has also robbed me of joy in my life by being a chronic worrier. I have had repeated dreams with anxiety themes in them. One such recurring dream was that I was back in college. I had signed up for several classes. One day I remember that I have forgotten to attend those classes. I ask myself, "Did I drop those classes?" I cannot remember. I panic and wake up. For years I had those dreams until I began to practice what Paul exhorts us to do in Philippians 4:6-7. After several years of repeated practice, I have noticed that those dreams have all but ceased. I have also noticed that I no longer panic in real life situations the way I used to in the past. When a worrisome situation arises I now experience a sense of calmness in my heart as I deal with the situation. It is a permanent change. It does not mean that I never experience anxiety any more. But when I do experience anxiety, there is a sense of peace in my heart that enables me to say, "It is well with my soul", as described by Horatio Spafford who wrote the well-known hymn with the same title. It feels as if there is a wall of protection that has been built around my heart to keep it from experiencing the tyranny of panic attacks that I used to have in the past.

Discouragement and Depression

All of us get discouraged from time to time but many of us manage to bounce back, while some go into a prolonged period of discouragement, leading to depression. A person should seek professional help when severely depressed. However, there are additional things that can be considered as well, particularly as relates to prevention of depression.

Depression can be caused by physiological factors or by psychosocial factors. Frequently it is caused by a combination of the two. Antidepressant medications are used to deal with the physiochemical aspect of depression, while *talk therapy* is designed to address the cognitive and emotional aspects. The Bible also offers certain principles that would be helpful to deal with depressive tendencies caused by depression-bound thinking patterns. It would not be wise, nor is it recommended, for a person to rely on the Bible alone and neglect obtaining professional help when struggling with depression. Biblical teachings, however, can be helpful in preventing and ameliorating depression.

Depressive moods involve negative thought patterns. When negative and destructive thoughts are allowed to continue without being redirected, we invariably come to the conclusion that we are worthless as human beings. When negative thinking is allowed to continue unchecked, we often end up in "a dark pit with no way out", resulting in a state of depression. When a person is caught in the grip of depression, it is no longer possible to simply "snap out of it." Unless depression is brought on suddenly by physiological factors or by a sudden traumatic event, the depressed person most likely has been engaging in a depressive pattern of thinking over a long period of time.

Most of us are not taught the art of being able to identify danger signs of going into depression through negative thinking. Depression comes from loss of faith. It stems from the loss of one's ability to believe and hope. The Bible has much to say about faith. But when a depressed person wistfully speaks of wishing to have faith, it sounds so hollow. Faith as a mere intellectual concept can do little to help a person who is deeply depressed.

Faith, if it is going to be of help, must be lived in our day-to-day experience. Faith is characterized by persistence. "Ask, seek and knock", said Jesus in Matthew 7:7–8. We need to apply this principle at every turn. No matter what happens, do not give up. Do not give into the hopeless feeling no matter how dark the future may appear. Do not throw in the towels. Live one day at a time. Do not get into the habit of all or none thinking. Do not always expect favors or nice treatment from others. Don't be surprised or discouraged when you are not treated fairly. It serves no purpose to complain that life is not fair.

Using the parable of the persistent widow and the unjust judge (Luke 18:2–8), Jesus told the disciples that even the most uncaring public official could be moved to grant favors to the person who does not give up. If faith is going to be of significant help in times of crisis, it must be routinely developed in our daily struggles with challenges of life. We must practice it until it becomes part of our personality. We must deepen it through every crisis we face. Negative and catastrophic thinking must be challenged at every turn. Our mind must be trained to think realistic thoughts. We have a tendency to slip into thinking based on fantasy rather than reality. Fantasies tend to be either catastrophic or utopian. Reality is neither. Faith squarely faces reality, makes peace with it and looks for possibilities it offers.

Faith must not only be persistent but also surrendered if it is going to be helpful in a time of crisis. There is no spiritual depth greater than that of total surrender to the sovereign, wise and loving God. The prophet Habakkuk experienced it when he learned of the impending destruction of the city of Jerusalem by the Babylonian army in the seventh century BC. He was horrified when he heard of the invading army that was to ravage the holy city. He was mystified when he learned that God was going to allow it to happen. But instead of getting angry or depressed, he learned to surrender himself to the Lord who alone could see the larger picture. "Though the fig tree does not bud and there are no grapes on the vines, though the olive crop fails and the fields produce no food, though there are no sheep in the pen and no cattle in the stalls, yet I will rejoice in the Lord; I will be joyful in God my Savior. The Sovereign Lord is my strength; he makes my feet like the feet of a deer, he enables me to go to the heights" (Habakkuk 3:17-19 NIV).

In the face of a looming calamity Habakkuk was totally powerless to do anything about it, except to complain to the Lord at first. But by surrendering himself to the all-wise God, Habakkuk was able to turn this very depressing prospect into an adventure-like experience to wait and see what the Lord was going to do. Surrendered faith does not lead to depression or despair; it leads to quiet anticipation with excitement.

Depression may also stem from hidden anger. It is said that nice and quiet people often harbor deep anger inside them. *Nice people* can be easily walked on without protests. A life-long pattern of such behavior can create hidden anger and resentment in a person, leading to depression. Most of the time such individuals are not aware of the anger inside. It was not until some perceptive patients in a psychiatric hospital pointed it out to me that I began to notice the anger inside of myself. I have always been known to be a "nice person" and I intend to remain so because it is the way I am, though I was advised by well-meaning friends during the height of the "me first" cultural movement in the 70's and 80's that I should change and not be so nice. But I am also aware of the potential danger of hidden anger in myself. Therefore, every time I have a chance, I go before the Lord to ask the Holy Spirit to identify the hidden anger inside so that I can do some house cleaning.

Depression could be caused by sluggish metabolism. Thyroid problems could be related to depression, which is why it is important to seek medical evaluation when depressed. It is not uncommon for people to drink a cup of coffee in the morning before they can get going for the day. I used to drink coffee but I stopped it when I discovered it was making me too anxious. After I stopped drinking coffee, I went through a period of feeling the blues. I felt what I could only describe as "an emptiness in my bones", especially on Monday mornings. I would pray that the Lord would take away this terrible feeling but it did not go away. Some days I would dread the thought of getting up in the morning. I began to give this feeling of emptiness to the Lord. I did not try to get rid of it. I simply turned it over to the Lord, remembering His words, "Come to me, all you who are weary and burdened, and I will give you rest" (Matthew 11:28 NIV). The empty feeling did not go away but it became more bearable. It was as if the Lord was saying to me, "I am not going to take the burden away from you but I will make it easier for you to carry." As I continued this practice, the feeling of depression eventually left me. For many years now I can no longer recall getting up in the morning with a sense of emptiness. Now I wake up every morning with a sense of fullness in my heart.

Depression is often accompanied by a sense of guilt. When we are guilty of having hurt someone, we need to take a corrective action as soon as possible. It may involve asking for forgiveness from the offended party. It may also involve changing some of our own behaviors, accompanied by a resolve not to repeat them. The guilt may also be related to having hurt ourselves or having grieved the Lord in some way. If a specific issue is identified, it needs to be dealt with, followed by repentance and/or forgiveness. We can learn not to make the same mistake twice, though we will probably make new ones, as noted by Mark Twain who quipped, "Don't make the same mistake twice; make new ones." The Lord will continue to help us "clean house" by providing forgiveness and cleansing (I John1:8-9).

For individuals with depression-proneness, the case is not so easily closed. The feeling of guilt continues to gnaw at their heart. They continue to feel the need for further acts of atonement. If they are Christians, they know in their minds that Jesus died on the cross for the forgiveness of their sins. But they do not *feel* forgiven even after repeated confessions of their sins. It was said of Martin Luther that as a monk he felt burdened with a persistent sense of sin and guilt. He dutifully engaged in acts of penance and atonement day after day until he finally understood the meaning of "The just shall live by faith." When he finally realized that he was forgiven by faith, it was said that he rose from his knees and ran down the steps, on which he had been climbing on his knees as an act of penance, shouting, "I am free. I am free, indeed."

For years I felt guilty inside. I felt that I always had to walk on egg shells so I would not offend others or displease the Lord. I had to be ever so careful to walk the narrow path and not step out of boundaries. But the word of God gradually set me free from the bondage of guilt. Now I not only believe but also *feel* the truth of the statement of Paul who said, "Therefore, there is now no condemnation for those who are in Christ Jesus" (Romans 8:1 NIV). But it took me many years to arrive at this point. I continued to live by faith and not by feelings but it was not always easy. Sometimes I had to pretend I was forgiven and act as if I was forgiven, though I did not feel forgiven. According to Dietrich Bonhoeffer, the Bible declares that our sins are forgiven through Christ, whether we feel it or not. There are many Christians who continue to live as if Christ never died for their sins because they rely on their feelings. I believe that Satan, our enemy, wants us to continue to believe in his lie to keep us from being set free.

Depression and joy cannot co-exist. When one comes in, the other goes out. It has been said there is a difference between happiness and joy. Happiness is dependent on the circumstances, while joy is not. Christians are admonished to rejoice always regardless of the circumstances. We cannot rejoice when circumstances are not good, unless we learn to give thanks in all circumstances, including *bad* circumstances. We cannot give thanks when circumstances are not favorable, unless we recognize the wisdom of God and trust in His sovereignty. Once again, surrender is the key. The Lord is infinitely wiser than we are. We can surrender our lives to Him and rejoice. When we are able to give thanks, joy will be restored and depression will take a back seat.

Thanksgiving and despair cannot co-exist. Ideally we should be able to manage depression by learning to give thanks but some of us may not be able to do it so easily, in which case seeking professional help is highly recommended. I believe God calls some people to become doctors, psychologists and counselors by gifting them to do what they do. God uses those professionals to bring healing to people who suffer from depression. The healing professional does not need to be a Christian, though a Christian therapist would be better able to understand what a Christian struggles with. A Christian therapist would be aware of the benefits of applying certain Biblical principles in the healing process. A Christian therapist would be able to address the problem of depression from a wider perspective, including the spiritual dimension in addition to the biological, psychosocial and cultural factors. But the most important consideration in choosing a therapist is how one can relate to the therapist. If you feel comfortable with your therapist and feel you can trust him or her, I would say you have made a good choice.

Depressive feelings are always unpleasant and painful. Therefore, we have a tendency to think that they are bad and should be rid of at any cost. However, depressive feelings are not completely without merit. There are benefits that come from depression that cannot be obtained any other way. The pole opposite of depression is *mania* which is an extremely elevated emotional state. A person in a manic state is unable to learn anything with deep meaning. Only a person who is in some emotional pain is able to understand deep things of life. King Solomon, one of the wisest people in history, noted, "Sorrow is better than laughter because a sad face is good for the heart" (Ecclesiastes 7:3 NIV). Some people go through *the dark night of the soul* which is a prolonged period of deep depression. Despite the best efforts made by the most competent psychiatrists and psychologists, deep depression can persist. The most important thing that a therapist can do in such cases is to keep the depressed person safe from self-harm by managing to keep the emotional pain within tolerable levels by whatever means available, while the depressed person works through the most delicate personal issues that need to be dealt with and eventually overcome. Depression is treatable. And there are Biblical materials that can be of help, as noted above.

Frustration, Anger and Resentment

Anger is often triggered by a frustrating experience. Frustration tolerance levels vary from one person to the next, just as depression-proneness varies from one person to another. Anger-proneness can also differ from one individual to another. Some people are "wired" to be quick tempered. How a person was raised will also affect the way he or she handles anger later in life.

According to the Bible, anger can be constructive or destructive. Anger can be used to bring about desirable changes or it can be used to injure people. Destructive anger is more noticeable and more frequently experienced in our lives. Anger can lead to physical injuries and even to murder. Anger can also cause emotional injuries. Contrary to the popular saying that words cannot hurt as much as sticks and stones, words expressed in anger can leave deep scars on the psyche of the recipient of such words. Civility is rapidly declining in our society and people seem to feel entitled to express unbridled anger without any hesitation or restraint. The pop psychology of the mid-20th century which condoned and even encouraged unbridled expressions of anger as a healthy way for a person to grow has no doubt contributed to the current state of affairs. "Let it all hang out" was the battle cry of that era which had originally come out as a reaction to what was perceived to be an overly restrictive way of life in the previous generations, which was thought to contribute to the development of neurosis in people. I think initially it had some merit but there is no doubt that the pendulum has swung too far to the other side, causing serious damages in our society. We hear news of people getting seriously injured from "road rage" incidents. We hear of children being bullied with serious consequences. There is a dire need for us to return to a more civilized way of life.

The Bible exhorts us to forsake destructive anger (Psalm 37:8). The Bible also reminds us that anger does not produce the righteous life God desires (James 1:20). I do not consider myself to be an angry person but I have had my share of anger until I realized that I needed to address how I dealt with anger in my life. When I address anger management issues in my counseling practice, I remind people of the value of restraining angry outbursts. Under the influence of our entertainment media which often glorifies violence, some of us may be inclined to think that a man (or even a woman) who uses explosive anger and aggression to solve problems is a hero to be emulated. But I am reminded of the wise advice given by King Solomon that a man who controls his anger is stronger than a warrior who conquers a city (Proverbs 16:32). There is a dire need to promote the value of restrained anger.

We are not always aware of the subtle anger accumulating in our heart as we encounter various obstacles in the course of our daily activities. The anger hidden inside of us can explode at a person or a situation that did not cause the anger, which is why it is important that we regularly examine our heart to see if there is any anger festering from unresolved issues we carry inside of ourselves. "Do not let the sun go down on your anger" was the advice given by the Apostle Paul because unresolved anger can be cleverly used by our enemy, Satan, to cause havoc in our lives (Ephesians 4:26-27). When we search our heart and find anger inside, we may be able to resolve it by confessing it. But if we cannot resolve it then and there, at least we should be aware of it so that we will not displace our anger on an innocent bystander.

There are daily irritations that can trigger angry reactions. For example, many of us who drive on congested city streets and crowded highways experience irritation and anger when other drivers cause inconveniences for us. I used to tailgate slow drivers to let them know I was irritated with them. But the Lord gave me an experience one day, which changed my attitude completely. We had just moved to a new neighborhood and I was still learning to maneuver my way around the nearby freeway system. One morning I was getting off one freeway to get on another freeway. I was driving along the off-ramp when I noticed a car close behind me. I sensed the driver wanted me to move over into the outer lane so that he can pass me on my left side. However, I saw a merge sign ahead, which meant that just a few yards ahead the two-lane off-ramp will have only one lane. So I stayed in the left lane. The driver behind me became impatient and he sped past me on my right side, which did not bother me. The next moment as the two lane off-ramp was becoming one lane, the driver of the car who had just passed me put on his breaks just a few feet ahead of me. I luckily managed to avoid a collision. The next moment the driver took off with his middle finger in the air in an obscene gesture. I became furious. I wanted to report him. I looked around for the highway patrol car I had spotted just a few moments ago but it was nowhere to be found. I was very angry. Then suddenly a thought popped into my head that I should pray for this driver. Perhaps no one had ever prayed for him before and the Lord wanted me to pray for this man. For the next few moments I literally prayed for my "enemy." When I was done praying, my anger was gone and the rest of the day was not ruined. But there is more. Something happened to me that day. Ever since then I have noticed how much nicer California drivers have become. They no longer irritate me. My driving experience has become so much more enjoyable. Obviously California drivers have not changed. I believe the Lord used that incident to change me. Now I seldom get irritated by other drivers on the road.

Anger can be used constructively. Jesus drove out the merchants from the temple yard in anger to cleanse the temple from sacrilege. He angrily denounced the religious leaders of His day for their hypocrisy. There are many people who engage in fighting against injustice and needless human suffering, motivated by a deeply felt anger against such evils. Such use of anger is constructive. Martin Luther King Jr.'s fight against racism has often been cited as an example. It is constructive anger that causes us to confront evils, injustices and wrongs in society. It is constructive anger that energizes us to confront what is harmful and destructive. But even constructive anger can easily turn into destructive anger unless we carefully examine it with the help of the Holy Spirit. Bombings of abortion clinics by those who oppose abortion would be an example of constructive anger turned destructive. Unbridled anger cannot be used constructively. Such anger may frighten and force people into conformance temporarily but no lasting change is unlikely to occur. Only disciplined anger can bring about constructive and genuine changes.

Resentment is anger gone underground. Unresolved anger can fester in our heart and turn into resentment. Strong resentment can turn into hatred. Resentment and hatred can poison us from within. Resentment harms the person who is doing the resenting and not the person who is the object of the resentment. The best remedy for resentment is forgiveness. But forgiveness is not easily achieved. We do not have within us what it takes to truly forgive others who offend us. We need to go outside of ourselves to find the resources needed to be able to forgive. There are many remedies offered in the Bible. The Apostle Paul reminds us that we can leave the matter with the Lord who promises, "Vengeance is mine; I will repay" (Romans 12:19 NKJV). If we can learn to let the Lord handle our grievances, we will be spared of the unnecessary burden of resenting someone when the matter cannot be resolved within our power. The most powerful example of forgiveness was offered by Jesus who, while dying on the cross, refused to be trapped in anger against the perpetrators of such a heinous act by saying, "Father, forgive them for they do not know what they are doing." A lesser person would have thought of a grand scheme of revenge with much destruction and bloodshed, which would have been justified. But Jesus came to show us a different way, the way of God, to deal with anger much more constructively. Again, the key is surrender. If we can learn to surrender ourselves to the Lord and choose to do it His way, we will have victory.

Relationship Difficulties

There are no perfect relationships just as there are no perfect human beings. We all need to learn ways to deal with problems that occur in relationships. When faced with relationship problems, we have a tendency to react to them the same way we react to any other problems. *Fight or flight* is our natural tendency to deal with any problem that presents itself. If we choose to fight in a tough relationship, we will argue and try to win the argument. When we sense that we will not be able to win, we might decide to avoid the problem by withdrawing. Neither option is effective in building good relationships. We must look for better ways.

The fight or flight instinct is operated by the emotional center of our brain. The emotional center of the brain is not able to come up with creative solutions to a problem. Only the thinking center of the brain is capable of producing more creative solutions. When faced with a difficult relationship, it is important that we take time to quietly reflect and think of effective ways to handle the relationship. We need to assess the situation and determine what is possible and what is not possible to do in the relationship. We would need to determine what the relationship is all about in terms of its nature, scope and meaning. In Romans 12:18 the Apostle Paul recommends, "If it is possible, as far as it depends on you, live at peace with everyone" (NIV). Paul is realistic about the fact that not all relationships will be smooth and harmonious. It requires wisdom on our part to be able to determine how far or how deep we can go in a relationship. Some relationships are casual and superficial and others go deeper. Some people are capable of going deep in a relationship and others are not. We need to cultivate the wisdom to know the difference. We can be spared of unnecessary pain by learning to stay within the boundaries of each relationship. Just as "water seeks its own level", each relationship settles in its own niche. It would be helpful to learn to accept each relationship as it comes.

There are bound to be conflicts and frictions in any relationship that lasts over a period of time. We need to learn the art of forgiveness if we are going to be able to manage the conflicts. Forgiveness is like a lubricant used in a motor. The lubricant keeps the motor from overheating and breaking down. Forgiveness provides the ability to overlook another person's imperfections. None of us are perfect, though we are sometimes under the illusion that we are. As soon as I remember that I am not perfect, it eases many of my relationship problems. When I remember that I am not perfect, I become more humble and can more readily forgive another person.

Sometimes we expect too much from a relationship and we end up being frustrated because the other person is not able to meet all of our expectations. We must realize that no human being can meet all of our needs at all times. Some people can meet some of our needs and others can meet other needs we have. There are some needs that no one else but God can satisfy. Some might feel that they can trust no one but God as a result of having been hurt or disappointed by people. But we must not stay there because we are designed to be social beings in need of human contact. Even hermits need some human contact to remain human. All of us need to continue to learn more effective relationship skills. Every difficult relationship presents an opportunity for us to develop more refined relationship skills.

Some people are hesitant to open up to others for fear of being hurt or disappointed. In order for us to be able to open up to others despite the fear of possible rejection, we must learn to love with *agape* love. Agape love is the unconditional love of God which keeps on loving regardless of the response received. It is the love that goes beyond the fear of rejection. We need to learn to love others without the fear of rejection if we are going to be emotionally healthy. In I Corinthians 13, which is known as the "love chapter", the Apostle Paul describes agape love. Agape love is characterized by patience and kindness. It "does not insist on its own way" and it "never ends." People who are able to love others with agape love are not afraid to love. Their love may not be reciprocated but they do not remain discouraged and lonely very long before they can rebound. Agape love can be developed with practice. People who are deeply grounded in Jesus Christ can continue to mature in their ability to love because the Holy Spirit will continue to prompt them to grow in love. But we cannot love people with agape love in our own strength; we need the Lord's help every step of the way to motivate us to keep on loving. People who are able to love with agape love are attractive and they do not lack friends. (Further discussion will follow in the section addressing "Agape Therapy" in Chapter Four.)

Perhaps the greatest challenge comes to us as Christians when we find ourselves at odds with another Christian. When dealing with non-believers, it may not be difficult to say, "Forgive them for they do not know what they do." But when we are dealing with a Christian brother or sister we might be inclined to say, "He/she should know better." This line of reasoning makes it difficult for Christians to forgive one another.

It is significant that Jesus told His disciples to love one another "even as I have loved you" (John 13:34). He did not say, "Love one another as you would love yourself." Self-love has limits. There are times when we might say, "I don't even love myself anymore." If we are going to be able to love a Christian brother or sister who offends us, we will need stronger motivation than self-love. We need a clear command from the Lord to love *as He loved* us. The Apostle John gave us a strong challenge when he said, "If anyone says, 'I love God', and yet hates his brother, he is a liar. For anyone who does not love his brother whom he has seen cannot love God whom he has not seen" (I John 4:20 NIV). Paul and Barnabas had a sharp disagreement over Mark when Paul did not consider him to be trustworthy and they parted company when they could not agree (Acts 15: 36-40). But Paul did not continue to have ill feelings about Mark, as evidenced by his later statement in II Timothy 4:11, in which he commends Mark (and Barnabas by implication) as "being helpful in my ministry." Sometimes the Lord uses people's different perspectives as a means of sending people in different directions to accomplish His purposes and we need not hold animosities toward our brothers and sisters who may disagree with us. I believe the Lord sometimes creates differences among us to spread us out into different parts of His kingdom and we need to learn not to take it personally when it occurs.

Challenges in Marriage

Until about the middle of the 20th century, the divorce rate among Christians in America was lower than that of the non-Christian couples. Today, however, the divorce rate is about the same for Christians and non-Christians alike. I believe the main reason for the high divorce rate is the prevalent belief that one should not tolerate pain if there is a way out of it. When marriage causes pain, people are tempted to believe they should get rid of the pain by ending the marriage. This simplistic approach does not solve the problem and some people go through multiple divorces leaving emotional wreckages behind. I have found that committed Christian couples do better when they are willing to work through the pain on the strength of their commitment to the Lord and to each other. In their humanness they may feel divorce may be an easy way out but their commitment to the Lord keeps them from bailing out.

Through trial and error some couples make it but others do not. I would highly recommend Christian marriage counseling for couples struggling in their marriage. I would also recommend pre-marital counseling for couples contemplating marriage so that they can prepare themselves for what lies ahead. All marriages go through painful stages but there are ways to lessen the pain by learning a few important principles.

First and foremost, we must stop trying to change our spouse. It has been found that happily married couples are those who do not try to change each other (3). "If only my spouse would change, I would be happy" is the most commonly heard complaint in marriage counseling. It is human nature to want to change one's spouse when there is a conflict. But this is a dead-end approach. It will either escalate into a bigger fight or one partner may decide to withdraw to keep the peace. But the issue will resurface in the same way or in a different context and the conflict will continue. There is a better way. We can stop trying to change our spouse by changing ourselves. We cannot change our spouse but we can change the way we respond to our spouse. The first thing we need to do is stop talking and start listening to our spouse and try to understand what our spouse is trying to say. We may not agree with what our spouse is saying but first we need to understand and affirm what is being said by our spouse. When we do not feel understood, negative emotions are aroused and rational conversation is difficult. But when we feel our opinions have been heard and affirmed for what they are, we are better able to engage in more rational conversation. The Apostle James reminds us that we need to "be quick to listen, slow to speak and slow to become angry" (James 1:19b NIV). When we are able to listen to our spouse and try to be careful not to contradict or disagree right away, a more productive conversation can follow.

Secondly, we need to learn to communicate with the "I-message." If it is important that we try not to change our spouse, how can we bring up issues that we happen to disagree on? All couples have differences in personality, family background, upbringing, personal habits and tastes and other factors that give rise to differences that can be annoying to each other. Initially those differences do not bother the couple when they are "in love" but sooner or later the differences will begin to annoy them. For a while they may try to ignore those annoying differences by trying to be patient but eventually they have to address it. Couples often use the word "always" or "never" when they try to communicate to their spouse about something that bothers them. Couples complain to each other by saying, "You *always* do that!" or "How come you *never* do that?" Those are emotionally charged expressions that arise out of accumulated frustrations over issues that have not been resolved. Trying to resolve the issue by making those statements of accusatory nature will only drive a wedge between the spouses.

A better way to communicate is to use the I-message rather than the you-message. Instead of saying, "Why do you always do that?", one could say, "I do not like it when you do that" or "I wish you would not do that." When we use the I-message, we can avoid an argument because there is not much to argue about a statement that is owned by the speaker. An I-message can make a clear statement about how the speaker feels without making assumptions about the listener. But when we use the you-message, it is bound to be met with a defensive rebuttal, followed by a lengthy argument because we are making assumptions about our spouse, which are not always accurate.

It is also recommended that after we make an I-statement we drop the matter and stop repeating the statement before it turns into *nagging*. When we make a clear I-statement, the information can be registered in the mind of the hearer but when it is followed by nagging, the information is more likely to be rejected. Some people might feel that they must repeat the statement to make sure that the other party hears it. The rationale behind it is understandable but nagging seldom works. When our spouse is unable to respond to our request even after it has been clearly stated with an I-statement, it would be more productive to ask ourselves how we could learn to accept our spouse's inability to respond than keep on hammering on the issue. When we stop forcing the issue, our spouses sometimes can respond better.

Thirdly, it is important to bring up the matter as soon as possible before it becomes deeply entrenched in the interaction pattern of the couple. When we can address the matter before the resentment builds up, it can be more easily resolved. "Do not let the sun go down on your anger", said the Apostle Paul (Ephesians 4:26-27). Frequently too much time has gone by and the matter is deeply entrenched in the mind of the spouse, making it difficult to calmly discuss it even with the use of an I-statement. If the matter has become a sensitive issue and it is too difficult to talk about it without an argument, we need to address it in our own quiet time with the Lord. We need to ask the Holy Spirit to reveal to us why the matter is so important. Frequently there is a long history behind it, deeply buried in our memory and hidden from our immediate awareness. But if we repeatedly focus on it in our quiet time with the Lord we might be able to gain some insight into the matter. It would also be helpful (and recommended) for the couple to seek marriage counseling as soon as possible if the problem does not go away. As with any illness, the longer we wait to see a doctor, the more complicated the problem can become. An ideal approach would be for a couple to have pre-marital counseling in which they are coached on how to communicate without trying to change each other and receive periodic *tune-up sessions* after they tie the knot until they can more skillfully learn the basic art of effective communication in marriage.

In some cases, however, the matter may never be resolved. Your spouse may not be able to understand your rationale. And your spouse may not be able to explain why he/she is not able to understand it. When that should be the case, it would be advisable that we learn to accept it and not try to change our spouse as long as the issue is not something unethical or dangerous. There are different ways of thinking and different ways of doing things. Neither one is right or wrong; they are just different. In fact, it is possible that the Lord brought you and your spouse together so that your horizons may be expanded. I am a logical thinker and my wife is an intuitive thinker. There were times in the past when the differences between us bothered me but now I realize that the Lord has brought us together so that my mind can be stretched and expanded for my benefit. I have gained deeper insight and wider perspectives on life through my wife. I think I have become a better person as a result of interacting with my wife whose personality is different from mine.

Challenges in Parenting

Parenting can be a daunting task. There are many helpful books and other resources available on the subject of parenting but we never seem to feel competent enough when it comes to parenting. How many parents would be able to say with confidence that they have done all the right things with their children and if they were to do it all over again they would do it exactly the same way? Even the parents whose children turn out fine by most standards would hesitate to take all the credit for it. Needless to say, the conflicted feelings of parents whose children go astray run deep. A generation or two ago it was the mothers who got most of the blame for children who turned out poorly. Today the fathers are no longer able to escape the blame.

There is no question that parenthood is a sensitive subject for many parents. Unfortunately, among some Christians how the children turn out is tacitly thought to be a measure of spiritual success for the parents. But there is no direct correlation between spirituality and how the children turn out. Obviously this line of reasoning is based on very simplistic thinking. It is akin to the notion that a "spiritual" pastor or a missionary should be able to build a large congregation. Some people erroneously interpret the verse in Proverbs where it says, "Train up a child in the way he should go and when he is old, he will not depart from it" (Proverbs 22:6 NKJV). Raising children is not as simple as molding clay into a bowl on a potter's wheel. Children are not born *tabula rasa* to be easily molded by the wishes of the parents. Biblical scholars agree that "to train up a child in the way he should go" means to mold the child in accordance with the in-born characteristics of each child. This is a Biblical prescription that should be followed but this is not a promise with guaranteed success because there are so many variables involved when it comes to raising a child.

Raising human beings is one of the most complex tasks known to us. The Bible provides very broad guidelines on how to raise children. Some Christian parents follow Biblical guidelines to raise their children who turn out well, while others who use the same guidelines experience heartache, guilt and shame when their children do not turn out the way they are expected to. Even the same parents may experience very different outcomes when they apply the same parenting principles with different children.

I have often wondered how God must have felt when Adam and Eve whom He created did not turn out the way they were expected to. Did God fail as Parent? Why did God let it happen? Why did He not correct it? Why did the children of Israel disobey God continuously? Why did God have to agonize over the rebellion of His children? There is a deep mystery about why God allowed the human race to turn out the way it did. Likewise, why do parents have to agonize over their children, especially wayward children? Obviously there are no simple answers to such questions. However, I have seen the *fruit* of such pain and suffering in the lives of many parents.

When we talk about parenting, we often focus on helping children grow and neglect the subject of helping parents grow as they engage in the difficult (and sometimes impossible) task of parenting. I firmly believe that the Lord gives us our children so that we may grow as parents just as much as our children do. Through the challenge of raising children parents can learn to experience the grace of God much more deeply. They can experience God's forgiveness for their sense of failure. They can learn to trust God and live one day at a time. They can also learn to be more compassionate toward others who struggle and fail.

Most parents manage to survive the storms and breathe a sigh of relief when they see their children coming out of the teenage years unscathed. But some are not so lucky. Their children get into some serious trouble. The agony and pain of the parents whose children go astray can only be understood by those who go through similar experiences. But all parents, regardless of how their children turn out, continue to worry about their children in one way or another as long as they live. The saying "once a parent, always a parent" aptly captures the essence of the parental love that never dies in the heart of a parent.

In the Christian community, perhaps the worst pain is felt by the parents whose children get into drugs or turn out to be homosexuals. To the parents of those children the news of such revelations is like a sentence of death. They are no longer able to hold highly-esteemed positions in the church. They feel like marginal people. Some leave the church, unable to bridge the chasm that has been unintentionally created between them and others who have not had similar experiences. But others go deeper and experience the grace of God in a way that would not be possible any other way.

For those who go deeper, the stereo-typical idea of being a Christian is transformed into a new one with much more solid meaning. They are no longer afraid of others who may not understand how they feel. They realize this is a cross that the Lord has given them to carry. They are not going to run away from it. They are going to do whatever they can to normalize their lives and live as fully as they can. They are going all the way with Christ by learning to grow through the *thorn in the flesh* experience which is not going to go away any time soon. There is a low-grade pain ever present in their heart. But the grace of God is richly available to sustain them. Some day when they are sufficiently healed of their scars, they can be used in a special way to minister to those who may be called the untouchables in society but who are just as precious in the Lord's eyes as anyone else.

Being able to talk to someone about the pain of parenthood in a non-judgmental atmosphere would be very helpful. The setting could be in a group or with an understanding individual who can listen. If it is in a group setting it should be built around a spirit of humility and not of competitiveness. In the context of a church the values shared by the participants would be similar but the participants must be sensitive not to boast about their children in the presence of others who cannot do the same with regards to their children. Agape love says, "I value you unconditionally as a person." How one's children turn out has nothing to do with the value of the parent as a person. Of course there are technical parenting skills that a parent can acquire to become a better parent. But the value of the parent as a person and his or her parenting skills must be clearly separated.

I believe that the Lord *loans* our children to us for a while so that we may grow in our ability to trust Him and experience His grace more deeply. In the final analysis our children are not ours; they belong to the Lord. I believe that the Lord in His great wisdom helps us parents grow along with our children as we struggle as parents.

The Problem of Aging

We live in a society with a self-defeating attitude toward aging. When we are young, we are told we are "too young." When we reach forty years of age, we are told we are "over the hill." Many people do not want to admit they are over thirty-nine years of age. It is not considered a polite thing to ask people over thirty how old they are. I once heard a radio talk show host who was describing some difficulty his aging mother was facing. He ended his remarks by screaming on the air, "Don't get old. It's a terrible thing to get old." It is a no-win situation because everyone grows old whether we like it or not. I was fortunate to be born in Japan at a time when elders were respected. I am also fortunate to have learned that in the Bible no one retired even at an old age. The Bible exalts old age by saying, "Grey hair is a crown of glory; it is attained in a righteous life" (Proverbs 16:31 NIV). In the Bible, people of all ages, both young and old, are valued. Even though I have been spared of having a strong prejudice against aging, I was being subtly influenced by the surrounding cultural sentiment against aging until a few years ago when I was introduced to the "sage-ing movement" which originated in the Jewish community.

Rabbi Zalman Schachter-Shalomi, in his book *From Age-ing to Sage-ing: A Revolutionary Approach to Growing Older*, discusses how we can enjoy life in our senior years by being able to reap the fruit of the long years of life experience. He talks about how life can be divided into three stages, childhood, adulthood and *elder-hood*. He does not specify the age range for each of the three stages. Applying it to my own life, I would say my childhood was from age one to twenty, my adulthood from twenty-one to sixty, at which point I entered my elder-hood. Looking back, I can truly say that I did not really begin to *live* until I was sixty years of age. Elder-hood represents the golden years of life. I am now truly enjoying my life to the full. Additionally the Lord has blessed me with good health and I try to maintain a healthy life style, which enhances my enjoyment of life.

As *elders* we are not here to compete with younger persons but to make our contributions to society with the wisdom gained as a result of aging. As we grow older, our physical capabilities decline as well as certain mental capacities. For example, I can no longer perform simple mathematical calculations in my mind as quickly as I did when I was younger. And of course

I can no longer engage in the physical activities the way I did when I was younger. However, my ability to think *globally* has greatly improved. I can now look at situations with wider and deeper perspectives than I did when I was younger. In the sageing movement, elders are encouraged to provide coaching and mentoring to the younger generations. Elders can also provide positive role models for younger persons to emulate. The late John Wooden would be a great example but we need not be famous to do the same for the people in our own lives who look to us for a role model.

Chapter Four

Continuing To Grow Through Emotional And Spiritual Challenges

Struggling with Doubt

To many of us "Doubting Thomas" is no stranger. We need to see before we can believe. This is how we are wired. We rely on our five senses to learn about the world. Empirical experiences through the five senses give us the most basic knowledge of our world. Infants learn about their world through touch, smell, taste, sound and vision. Through repeated experiences with the use of the five senses, we gradually develop logical reasoning, based on the interface of cause and effect. As we grow older, we continue to develop logical reasoning which includes the belief "seeing is believing." This belief generally keeps us in good standing with our world. This is how we are created to be able to function in the physical world.

With the use of our senses and logical reasoning, we gradually create in our mind an image of the world we live in, which is sometimes referred to as a *worldview.* Our worldview is always subject to modifications with new information we receive. The Apostle Thomas had a worldview based on his life experiences that taught him that the dead just do not come back to life. When he heard the Jesus had been raised from the dead, he was skeptical because this was new information to him. His skepticism was warranted. But when he actually saw the resurrected Jesus with his own eyes, he was challenged to drastically modify his worldview (John 20:24-29).

Most of us living with a rational/scientific worldview have difficulty believing supernatural events. Many things in the Bible involve supernatural events which cannot be easily understood with the use of rational thinking alone. It requires faith to understand and benefit from the Bible. It requires faith to believe in the existence of God (Hebrews 11:6). Faith is the most fundamental human behavior, without which life is impossible. Every day all of us, including the atheists, live by faith, though we may not think in those terms. We live by faith believing that tomorrow will come. We live by faith trusting that the ground we stand on will not give away. This is not blind faith. It is based on sufficient evidence, based on our daily experiences. Through repeated experiences with our world, we can safely assume tomorrow will be here, even though there is no absolute guarantee of that. All of us live by faith every day without thinking about it. But when we are told that we must believe in God by faith, we face a challenge because we have never seen God. We can believe tomorrow will come because we have seen tomorrow come repeatedly. But how can we believe in the existence of God whom we have never seen? This is a dilemma for many of us. Are we expected to believe in God blindly? It is true that there are countless billions of people throughout history who would testify that it is safe to believe in God, but there are others who would disagree.

I do not believe, however, that intellectual reasoning alone will ever bring people to saving faith in God. I believe it is possible to acknowledge the existence of God by intellectual reasoning, following, for example, the arguments advanced by the proponents of the Intelligent Design theory. In fact it would require greater faith to believe that this amazing universe came into being by pure chance than to believe in the existence of an intelligent Supreme Being who created the universe. I do not believe, however, anyone can come to acknowledge Jesus Christ as Lord without being prompted by the Holy Spirit (I Corinthians 12:3). When we begin our faith journey, we are challenged to deepen our faith at every turn as we struggle with the tension between faith and reason. Doubts about the Bible will be thrown at us by skeptics. Depending on our personal experiences, we may struggle with our own doubts. The human mind is an amazing apparatus. It is capable of a wide variety of thinking ranging from solipsism to positivism. We are capable of thinking that life is but a dream and that one day we will wake up from our dream to realize that it was only a dream. On the other hand, there are those who insist that only the things we can verify by the five senses are real. I believe the truth is somewhere between those two extreme views. We are capable of exercising imagination but we are also tempered with the ability to run reality checks. The challenge is how to balance the two. We are constantly challenged to make decisions, based on the interface between faith and reason.

When we engage in decision making, there are two errors we need to avoid. In the field of probability theory, those errors are known as Type I and Type II errors. Type I error occurs when we conclude something is true when it is not. The Type II error is to conclude something is not true when it is true. Scientific researchers are very careful to avoid the Type I error. Researchers are expected to take extreme caution to avoid making the Type I error to minimize the possibility of reporting false information, which exposes them to the risk of making the Type II error. They are so careful to avoid reporting false information that they frequently reject true information. This is acceptable and even expected in the field of scientific research. Unfortunately the same line of thinking is applied to critical examinations of Biblical materials. I believe Biblical truths are too often discarded as untrue by those who subscribe to narrow positivistic thinking. As a result, they miss out on the blessings that come from believing in the Bible as the revealed word of God.

The Power of Surrender

The Serenity Prayer, whose authorship is attributed to Reinhold Niebuhr, is well-known in the recovery circles. It provides helpful guidance to people, both Christians and non-Christians, who struggle with life's challenges. A popular version of it reads, "Lord, grant me the courage to change the things I can change, the serenity to accept the things I cannot change, and the wisdom to know the difference." When faced with a challenge, the usual human reaction is to try to change it, which requires courage and determination to accomplish. When the challenge turns out to be formidable, we need greater courage and resolve. The Bible is replete with stories and examples of people who conquered great obstacles with courage and faith (Hebrews 11). Secular history also abounds with stories of individuals and groups of people who overcame insurmountable odds with great courage. Need for courage to accomplish God's purpose in our lives is self-evident.

But what happens when the situation remains unchanged no matter how hard or how long we struggle to change it? The

Serenity Prayer suggests that we consider an alternative option of accepting the situation with serenity. How can we do it? It is natural for us to protest when we are forced to change our direction when we have been so focused on going in a certain direction. It is never easy to accept a course of action which is not to our liking. How can we do it? As Christians we have Biblical examples to learn from. In the story of Job, in the midst of his pain and agony, Job had the presence of mind to admit that God may not answer his prayer but he would still trust God (Job 13:15). Daniel and his friends had the boldness to say that even if God did not save them from death in the burning furnace, they would still not betray God (Daniel 3:16-18). Many of the saints of God whose heroic accomplishments are chronicled in the 11th chapter of Hebrews were willing to go all the way, though they did not see their promises fulfilled in their life time (Hebrews 11:13). The Apostle Paul learned to accept the *thorn on his side* with serenity, realizing that God had a more valuable lesson for him to learn than removal of his pain (II Corinthians 12:7-10). How were those individuals able to do what they did? How were they able to accept the situations they could not change? They all had faith in the wisdom and sovereignty of God. They were able to trust God with their lives and were willing to accept even the most unfavorable circumstances they found themselves in, knowing that there was more to come and that God was not yet finished.

Being able to trust is a basic human need. Without it we cannot live normal lives. People who experience severe abuse, neglect or betrayal as children or even later in life can have serious difficulty in trusting. The ability to trust is developed as we encounter and interact with trustworthy people. Since few of us have perfect childhood upbringings, many of us have some measure of difficulty in trusting. We all struggle with doubt at times. We go back and forth between faith and doubt, which is a normal human experience. There is a difference between intellectual ascent and trust. We may intellectually believe something to be true but when we are called on to act on it, we hesitate. There is a reason for this. Before we can believe something to be trustworthy, we must have sufficient evidence for it. A story is told of a skilled tightrope walker who walked across the Niagara Falls with a heavy load on his back. When he finished this great feat, the spectators applauded him. When he asked the spectators if they believed he could take a man on his back across the Niagara Falls, they responded affirmatively. However, when he asked for a volunteer, no one came forward. I am not sure if this is a true story but I have heard sermons preached with this story as an illustration to challenge people to have greater faith. Personally, however, I am glad no one volunteered to ride on the back of the trapeze artist. No one in his or her right mind would do such a reckless thing by choice. There is a difference between a leap of faith and naïve gullibility. A better illustration to use might be the case of air travel. Millions of people travel by air, though there are times when we experience moments of doubt about the safety of air travel when there is a report of a mishap. Why do we continue to fly in airplanes? Because there is sufficient evidence to believe that the airplane we fly in should safely take us to our destination. Countless millions of Christians throughout history have lived by trusting God and they would all testify that it was a good life and that if they were to do it all over again, they would not hesitate to do so. The one difference between air travel and living by trusting God is that air travel may be 99.9% safe, whereas living by trusting God is 100%

safe. Indeed, there are times and situations in our lives when we are unable to change unfavorable circumstances but if we learn to accept them with serenity, trusting in God's wisdom and sovereignty, we will be able to look back and agree with the Apostle Paul who concluded that "all things work together for good to those who love God, to those who are called according to His purpose" (Romans 8:28 NKJV). The fourth stanza of the classic hymn, "Amazing Grace", expresses this sentiment well:

> Through many dangers, toils and snares,
> I have already come,
> 'Tis grace that hath brought me safe thus far,
> And grace will lead me home.

The third point of the Serenity Prayer is the need for wisdom to know when to persist in trying to change the situation and when to stop. I think this is the most difficult part of the Serenity Prayer and it takes a life time to learn it. Every situation we face in life is different. We cannot automatically know when to persist and when to stop. The Christian life cannot be put on autopilot. We need to be in constant communication with God, the Father, who is our Great Pilot. Only He can tell us when to persist and when to stop and change direction. In my own life I have learned to rely on the inner prompting of the Holy Spirit and to discover God's will by following the doors that open and the doors that close. When a door opens I enter it if the Holy Spirit prompts me to do so. When a door closes, I wait and look for another door to open. I am finding this to be an exciting adventure. The key is surrender. Surrendering to God's will is the most important lesson we can learn. According to Hannah Whitall Smith, the author of *The Christian's Secret of a Happy Life,* surrender is the key to a meaningful and satisfying Christian life.

No doubt, there are people who would say that they have trusted God and ended up in disappointment. I believe people who are disappointed by God are those who have not yet learned the art of accepting things they cannot change with serenity. We may try to change unfavorable situations with courage and determination until we become exhausted. At this point we have a choice either to go away disappointed or go deeper by learning to surrender to the will of our heavenly Father by saying, "Not my will, but yours be done." God answers all of our prayers. His answer could be "yes", "no" or "wait." The problem with many of us is that we erroneously conclude God is not answering our prayers when His answer is "no" or "wait." When the answer is "yes", we rejoice but not much spiritual growth takes place. But when the answer is "no" or "wait", we agonize but we can go deeper to gain spiritual maturity. When God is silent, we have a choice either to walk away frustrated and cynical or go deeper. God, our heavenly Father, wants us to grow into spiritually mature adults but our human nature rebels against it, wishing to remain infantile or adolescent in our thinking. He does not force us to change but if we yield to Him by surrendering to His wise and sovereign will and follow Him one step at a time, we will be pleasantly surprised one day to find how far we have come in our ability to accept the things we cannot change and do so with serenity. When we look back on those experiences, we will discover that we have not only survived but thrived and spiritually grown as a result of those experiences. And if we live long enough, we will be able to thank God for all of the "no" and "wait" answers we received and truly marvel at His wisdom.

Living One Day at a Time

Jesus taught the disciples to live one day at a time, saying, "Therefore do not worry about tomorrow, for tomorrow will worry about itself. Each day has enough trouble of its own" (Matthew 6:34 NIV). Most of us can manage a problem or two at a time but when problems multiply on us it becomes more difficult. One way to prevent problems from multiplying is to live one day at a time.

Most of us live under the assumption that we are going to be around forever. But this is not realistic. Any of us can be taken away at any time. The Apostle James reminds us that life is like a mist, here now and gone the next moment (James 4:13-16). To realize the transitory nature of life on earth is not an escape; it is facing reality as it is. The realization of the transitory nature of life can help us gain a healthier perspective on life. It has been argued, and rightly so, that people must take responsibility to make plans for the future. The writer of Proverbs reminds us of the importance of preparing for the future by citing how the ants store their food in the summer (Proverbs 30:25). However, we are not to live in the future; we are to live in the present. It is easy to become so focused on the future that we neglect to live in the present. It is easy to have future plans with all kinds of *what if* scenarios and worries which can make us very stressed out. We need to develop the art of making responsible plans for the future, yet at the same time being able to live one day at a time without borrowing problems from tomorrow.

There is a wide-spread interest in the discussion of the end-time prophecies. I have seen two kinds of reactions among Christians who engage in discussing the "soon return" of the Lord. There are those who are comforted by the fact that Jesus is coming back, which encourages them to live each day fully for the Lord (I Thessalonians 5:11). And then there are those, especially among some young people, who get discouraged, saying, "If Jesus is coming back so soon, what would be the point of staying in school or getting married?" Throughout history there have been groups of people who sold their homes and left their businesses to go to the mountain top to wait for the soon return of the Lord. Such actions are based on complete misunderstanding of Biblical teachings and miss the point of the second coming of Christ. The Bible repeatedly exhorts us to be fully engaged in what we are called to do by and for the Lord (Matthew 24:45-46) because no one knows the exact time of Christ's return, except God, the Father in heaven (Matthew 24:36). It could be today, tomorrow, next year or a thousand years from now (II Peter 3:8). We must learn to develop the art of living one day at a time as if it was our last day on earth and at the same time live as if the world as we know it will continue to exist for another thousand years. Both are realistic and Biblical. If we follow those Biblical principles by living one day at a time, we will be able to live responsibly to care for the things we love but at the same time being spared of the unnecessary anxiety, stress and the burdens of life.

We need to develop the art of living one day at a time as if this was the last day of our lives on earth but at the same time be prepared to live out a long and fruitful life on earth until the Lord calls us home at a ripe old age or take us home sooner through an illness, accident or in a *rapture* as described by the Apostle Paul (I Thessalonians 4:13-18). How can we do this? How can we be prepared for all those different scenarios? On the one hand, there is no guarantee of life on earth for more than a few moments at a time. We are told that when our heart stops, it takes only about eight minute before the brain begins to die unless blood is supplied to the brain by an artificial means such as cardio-pulmonary resuscitation (CPR). If this is true I am only given absolute guarantee of my earthly life for about eight minutes at any given moment. How can we live a long and fruitful life on earth with such miniscule guarantee of life on earth? I am reminded of a soldier in combat who is under heavy enemy fire with no guarantee of life for more than a few seconds at a time but continues to persevere to survive to live, determined to see the day when he will be able to return home and see his loved ones. In order to survive the combat, the soldier must master the art of living one moment at a time but at the same time be prepared to live out the many remaining years of his life. A spiritually mature Christian can do the same but it takes consistent mental practice and discipline to achieve such mastery.

A Mark of Spiritual Maturity

We come into this world as infants but over time we grow to become mature adults. When we receive Jesus Christ as our Savior, we are spiritually born and begin our spiritual journey as infants in Christ. Over time we should grow spiritually as we read the Bible, receive spiritual instructions and learn to apply them in our lives. When infants do not grow, it is sad and could even be tragic. Stunted physical growth among children is rare. Lack of social, intellectual or emotional growth among children is more prevalent, which causes concerns for parents and others. Spiritual growth is more subtle and difficult to define. As Christians, we are expected to grow. Some people can remember when and how they became Christians but others do not, especially if they were raised in a Christian family and exposed to Christianity early in life. Regardless of how we become Christians, our developmental task is to grow as Christians. We should not remain spiritual infants. How can we grow spiritually and become mature Christians? There are different ways we can grow spiritually. In this book I have emphasized the importance of the basic spiritual disciplines of the Christian life, including applying the word of God, learning to interact with the Lord in prayer and being encouraged and supported in authentic Christian fellowship. But how do we know if we are growing? What are the marks of a spiritually mature Christian?

A major difference between a child and an adult is that an adult can do many things that a child cannot do. A child looks forward to the day when he or she will be able do all the things an adult can do. As we grow as Christians and become more adult-like, we will be able to do things that we could not do when we were less mature. I believe the Apostle Paul demonstrated an epitome of spiritual maturity when he wrote from a Philippian jail, "I can do all things through Christ who strengthens me" (Philippians 4:13). He faced incredibly difficult challenges in his life but he was able to overcome them by relying on Christ's strength. If we are going to become mature adult Christians, we will need to learn to rely on Christ to enable us to do the things that we cannot do in our own strength.

There are many things in my life which are challenging. My human tendency is to avoid them, which is tempting to do at times. If I avoid them I may experience a sense of relief but a quiet sense of discontent will follow as if the Holy Spirit is nudging me to reconsider my decision. When I realize I should not avoid it, I utter a short prayer, "Lord, I need your help; please help me" and then jump in. Amazingly, I have always been able to manage those difficult situations with favorable outcomes whenever I remember to call on the Lord for help. Sometimes, however, the matter is not that simple. There is a longer period of struggle I go through. It is usually related to an area in my life that is underdeveloped or damaged by a traumatic experience in the past. In my struggle I vacillate between a desire to face it and a desire to run away. If I decide to run away, I may feel a sense of relief but the Holy Spirit will quietly knock on my heart, reminding me that I can do all things through Christ who strengthens me. What I need to do is ask the Lord for help.

If I decide to take on the challenge but fail to call on the Lord for help, I will struggle in my own strength until I give up in defeat. But if I can remember to ask for help from the Lord, I can say with the Apostle Paul that I can indeed do all things through Christ who enables me to do so. It does not mean I am always successful but I can always try again until I do succeed. I believe a spiritually mature Christian is a man or a woman who has learned to rely on the Lord in every area of his or her life. It is not to say that we will no longer experience *fear and trembling* but there will be a sense of adventure and excitement as to how the Lord is going to help us deal with the challenges.

When the situation is extremely difficult, the temptation to run away can be very strong. When faced with a very complex and difficult situation, I struggle between a desire to avoid the challenge and a desire to face it. Am I willing to allow the Lord to stretch me beyond where I am? I vacillate. But in the end I can find the *peace of God* only when I decide to do it His way. I believe a spiritually mature Christian is a person who has learned to experience God's power being made perfect in one's weakness (II Corinthians 12:9). Sometimes when I experience my "world" crumbling, I feel a knot in the pit of my stomach.

I feel my strength leaving me, making me feel very weak. I feel lost until I remember I have an opportunity to experience God's power made perfect in my weakness. I remain in deep silence and wait for a direction from the Lord. This is how the Lord sustains me with His power when I become totally weak and helpless. He has never failed me and I do not think He ever will.

Our journey begins when we are willing to grow spiritually and emotionally. But the journey can be long and difficult. When the journey gets tough, we may tolerate it for a while. But when it gets tougher, we will be tempted to complain about our lot in life. We may question and even doubt if we are in God's will. We moan and groan and continue to suffer until we learn to *delight* in our weaknesses and difficulties as the Apostle Paul learned to do (II Corinthians 12:10). Until we learn to delight in our difficult situations, our journey will be an uphill battle. When we begin to accept the difficulties we are faced with, our journey will become less stressful. When we go a step further and learn to give thanks for the challenges we are faced with, our journey will become a deep learning and growing experience. I do not know how long it took Paul to reach the stage of being able to delight in his weaknesses but when he reached that stage, he found that the difficulties he faced in life worked for him rather than against him (Romans 8:28).

The journey will not always be smooth but a spiritually mature Christian is willing to stay on the path and is able to experience the fullness of God's grace. A spiritually mature Christian is no longer afraid of humiliation or failure by being able to fully accept the forgiveness and redemption so richly offered in Christ. Being able to fully immerse in God's grace is the key to spiritual growth. When I am going through a particularly long and difficult journey, I regularly take my eyes off the *things of earth* and bathe myself in God's grace, which renews me. When I do this, I can see God's will for my life more clearly. I am no longer afraid of feeling weak and helpless because when I feel vulnerable it gives me an opportunity to go deeper in my relationship with the Lord. And in the end the Lord always provides *a way of escape* with a new direction so that I am able to endure the trial in victory (I Corinthians 10:13). When the journey is tough, having a spiritually mature listening partner to interact with along the way is of great help, as discussed under "The Ministry of Listening" in Chapter Two.

Benefits of Suffering

Everyone seeks happiness. The United States Declaration of Independence which has had a world-wide influence in the field of political philosophy lists *pursuit of happiness* as an unalienable human right. But not everyone can find happiness as desired. Some people may never have a chance to experience much happiness. Others may find it but find it disappointing in the end. King Solomon pursued happiness through every human activity known to man but found that it was like *chasing after the wind*, meaningless and empty. Viktor Frankl who survived the Nazi concentration camp learned that the ultimate goal of life is not to find happiness but to find meaning. Not everyone can find happiness at all times but everyone can find meaning in all things, including suffering. There is nothing wrong with seeking happiness, which is a normal human desire. But the fact remains that no one can be happy at all times. Everyone will go through times of suffering in this life, unless perhaps one dies at a very young age. Is going through the experience of suffering a waste of time? Not so according to the Bible. The Bible makes it clear that suffering has a purpose. King Solomon found that sorrow is better than laughter, noting that sorrow is "good for the heart" (Ecclesiastic 7:3). How can sorrow be good for the heart? The heart is the deepest part of a person. The heart is touched by sorrow. Sorrow opens the door to the innermost part of a person to enrich it.

It has been said laughter is good medicine. Norman Cousins, in his book *Anatomy of An Illness*, describes how he was cured of an illness declared to be incurable by his doctors. He was able to heal himself by spending time laughing as he watched hilarious comedy films for days on end. "A cheerful heart is good medicine but a crushed spirit dries up the bones", observes the writer of Proverbs (Proverbs 17:22 NIV). Medical science is finding that a cheerful attitude elevates the serotonin and endorphin levels in the body, enhancing both mental and physical health. How can we have a cheerful attitude when we are suffering? The Apostle Paul exhorts us to "rejoice in the Lord always" (Philippians 4:4), which means we are to rejoice in all circumstances, including difficult ones. How can we rejoice in difficult situations? How can we rejoice in suffering? Humanly speaking, it makes no sense. But when we turn to the Bible, we discover we can rejoice in suffering because the Lord has a purpose for our suffering.

The Apostle Paul made a profound discovery. In his Second Letter to the Corinthians, Paul describes how even the most painful situation can prove to be an occasion to *rejoice* in the following ways. First, it can cause us to turn to the Lord to seek His help rather than continue to struggle relying on our own limited strength (II Corinthians 1:8-10). Secondly, having gone through the experience of being strengthened by the Lord, we can also provide comfort to those who are going through suffering. When we have gone through suffering and have come out in one piece by being sustained by the Lord, we are able to stand by another person going through suffering and offer comfort that we have experienced ourselves (II Corinthians 1:3-4). In those situations, we may not be able to think of the right words to say to comfort the person in suffering but our body language will communicate the peace and confidence we have in Christ, gained from our own experiences. Jesus Christ, the High Priest, is able to empathize with all of us because He experienced all of human suffering (Hebrews 4:14-16). He is described as the *man of sorrows* acquainted with grief (Isaiah 53:3). None of us will ever experience all of the pain Jesus bore. There is no pain that we experience that Jesus cannot understand. As we learn to endure our pain by being sustained by the Lord, we will be able to offer a sense of comfort and peace to those who are in pain. I have been told that plants grow more at night than during the day when the sun is shining. Likewise, we may need to experience going through the *dark night of the soul* ourselves at times in order to grow spiritually and become better equipped to understand the sufferings of others. A poem by Robert Browning Hamilton aptly describes how sorrow can be a beneficial human experience.

I walked a mile with Pleasure;
She chatted all the way;
But left me none the wiser
For all she had to say.

I walked a mile with Sorrow;
And never a word she uttered.
But, oh! The things I learned from her,
When Sorrow walked with me.

Such are the benefits of suffering. None of us will be spared of suffering if we live long enough in this life. But there is a way to endure it and even to benefit from it when we follow Biblical prescriptions. The longer we live in this world, the more suffering we will experience. If we allow suffering to weight us down, we can be beaten down and become cynical or even despairing. But if we allow the Lord to help us, we will be able to find meaning even in our suffering and grow spiritually and bring glory to God. When we surrender ourselves to the Lord, we will always find His grace to be sufficient.

Some critics of Christianity will dismiss such an approach as a case of masochism (pathological enjoyment of pain). Far from it. I believe it is a realistic but overlooked approach to the problem of pain. Emotional pain is real and we need to address it. The usual approach is to try to reduce it by physical or psychological means, which I whole-heartedly endorse. Advancements in psychiatry, psychology, counseling and other related disciplines give us options today to help us reduce emotional pain in our lives. When the pain is reduced it is easier for us to learn and grow through the pain. However, sometimes the pain is so deep and long-lasting that nothing seems to work. In such cases some people opt to seek relief from it by suicide. The Bible offers an alternative approach. Rather than trying to be rid of the pain which will not go away no matter what we do (short of suicide), the Bible shows us how to find meaning and purpose in it with God's help. The Apostle Paul went through such tremendous hardships in the province of Asia that he *despaired even of life* (suicidal thought), which led him to an amazing discovery of God's deeper purpose for his life. He realized he had an opportunity to completely rely on God and that if he survived he would be able to comfort others going through similar hardships (II Corinthians 1:3-11). Again the key is to totally surrender our will to the wise and sovereign plan and purpose of our heavenly Father. It may be said that *dying to self* (completely surrendering our ego to the Lord) can be an alternative to suicide.

The Power of Humility

The idea of humility has a negative connotation because it implies self-deprecation. Humility is not an inborn quality; it has to be learned. It is never easy to learn humility because it goes against our basic human nature which wants to assert itself. As we grow up, we are told that we need to learn to be humble in order to be able to function in society. In our socialization process we learn to put ourselves aside to please others. We may even learn to put ourselves down in order to gain the favor of another. People with good social skills have an ability to be humble; they know how to make the other person feel important with an attitude of selflessness. An attitude of humility helps to improve human relationships. But genuine humility is difficult to be attained and we sometimes settle with false humility. We may pretend to be humble in order to gain some advantage for ourselves. In some cases, we may even force ourselves to believe that we are of little value as human beings in order to rationalize an experience of failure. The rationale for this is, "If I cannot succeed, I must be no good." This line of reasoning will result in accumulation of self-hate, which can lead to depression. The opposite of humility is pride. In most societies pride is considered to be an admirable quality. A proud person feels confident and strong. The feeling of confidence is a good feeling. Therefore, pride is considered to be praiseworthy, whereas the idea of humility is a mixed bag at best.

The Bible talks about pride and humility. The Bible takes a different view of pride and humility from the way the world views them. According to the Bible, pride is one of the cardinal sins (Proverbs 6:16-19). Satan fell from heaven due to his sin of pride (Isaiah 14:12-15). We are warned, "Pride goes before destruction and a haughty spirit before a fall" (Proverbs 16:18 NIV). Why is it that the Bible warns against pride? I can think of several reasons. One reason is that pride makes us blind. When we are proud, we do not think we need to learn anything. When we are proud, we are puffed up. One of the characteristics of youth is pride. In our formative years, we sometimes develop an inflated view of ourselves, which needs to be adjusted through reality testing. When we use the word *pride* to refer to positive feelings we may have about certain things, such as our family, alma mater, or some progress we have made, we may not be off the mark. But when we go a step further and use the word to describe total independence without recognition of our dependence on God, we are in a danger zone, courting a fall. Pride can hinder development of deep relationships. It is difficult to feel close to a person who is full of pride and self-importance. Pride can also be a cover for lack of self-confidence. Pride is not all praise-worthy as touted by the world. When we are feeling proud, it gives us a good feeling but we need to examine ourselves to make sure that we are not standing on hollow ground that could crumble at any time.

According to the Bible, humility is more powerful than pride. Pride is built on man's self-efforts but Biblical humility comes from recognition of our dependence on God. Human pride is fragile; it can easily get hurt. It needs to be constantly guarded from forces that will try to pull it down. It takes constant vigil and energy to maintain pride, which can be stressful. Humility, on the other hand, needs no protection from destructive forces. Humility rests on the ground level with no danger of falling. However, we need to make a distinction between self-generated humility and Biblical humility. Self-generated humility is subject to self-deprecation, leading to low self-esteem. Biblical humility is born out of total recognition of divine sovereignty and is free from self-pity or self-hate. It is free from both self-generated grandiosity and self-pity. It recognizes divine reality and embraces it. The Apostle Paul was able to say, "I have learned the secret of being content in any and every situation, whether well fed or hungry, whether living in plenty or in want (Philippians 4:12b NIV). Paul was referring to material abundance or lack of it in this context but I believe it can also be applied to any situation we find ourselves in. A truly humble person in the Biblical sense cannot be destroyed because his/her ego has been totally surrendered to the sovereign will and purpose of the Lord. When fierce storms of life have passed, ripping apart one's dignity and pride, the humble person will still be standing ready to take the next step to accomplish God's ultimate purpose. Such is the power of humility.

Agape Therapy: A Christian Way of Being in this Broken World

If one were to summarize the teachings of the entire Bible in a few words, one might choose to quote, "Love the Lord, your God, with all your heart, soul and mind and love your neighbor as yourself", which is commonly known as the *Great Commandment* (Matthew 22:37-40). For a Christian who is looking for a practical way of living in the world, the Great

Commandment will provide a good foundation to build on. There are three parts to the commandment; loving God, loving one's neighbor and loving oneself (implied). The word *love* used here is a translation of the Greek word *agape* which refers to the unconditional love of God. Agape love is deeper than human love because it is based on commitment rather than on feelings which characterize human love. It is a love that is not dependent on the response it receives; it is a one-way love based on commitment and does not expect anything in return. When we live by agape love, our lives become more stable because we operate from the foundation of commitment rather than from human emotions. We live in a broken world and we all experience brokenness, for which we need healing. As a Christian counselor, I have found that living by agape love brings about deeper levels of healing than anything else available to us. Living by the essence of the Great Commandment might be called "agape therapy" as a distinctly Christian way of being in this broken world. Agape therapy enables us to give and receive healing in this broken world through the love of Christ. It is a way of living based on a practical and personal application of the Great Commandment by followers of Christ.

The Great Commandment begins with "Love God." How can we love God? The Apostle John reminds us that we love God because He first loved us (I John 4:19). It is not in our nature to love God. We can love God because He first loved us. God took the initiative to send His Son to die on the cross, demonstrating His love for us. When we understand how much God loves us, we can begin to love Him in return. The Bible which has been called "God's love letter to the human race" tells us that God loved us so much that He became a human being in the person of Jesus of Nazareth and died on a Roman cross for the forgiveness of our sins. God did all of this while we were being indifferent or even hostile toward God (Romans 5:8). Such is the extent of God's love for us. When we understand the extent to which God loves us, we are not only moved but also feel safe to respond to His love. The certainty of God's love is unmistakably shown throughout the Bible and it enables us to boldly trust in Him.

What does it mean to love God in response to His love? Jesus said, "If you love me, you will obey what I command" (John 14:15 NIV). To love God means to obey God and do what He wants us to do. How can we do this? When we realize how much God loves us, we can trust Him and begin to do what He wants us to do. When we decide to obey God, we are to do so with our *heart, soul and mind*, which is to say we are to obey God from the deepest part of ourselves. The deepest part of our personality is the *ego* which sits on the throne of our lives. We do not like our ego to be challenged. We want to be our own boss. We do not want anyone dictating to us what to do, including God. Ironically we forget that God is our Maker who knows us better than we know ourselves. God gave us the Bible which has been compared to the user's manual written by the manufacturer of an equipment. The word of God shows us how we are made and how we operate as delicate and complex human beings. It also shows us how we can be restored and made whole to function again when we break down. It shows us how we are to live to accomplish His purpose for our lives. For this to happen, we must be willing to obey God and follow His directions.

Sometimes we may hesitate to read the Bible because it causes feelings of discomfort just as we sometimes feel hesitant to go to a doctor for fear of being given some bad news. Truth hurts but it also heals. When I was a young Christian, a comment occasionally heard among my Christian friends was, "I hesitate to surrender my life to God because He might change my plans." I have had similar apprehensions over the years but fifty years later I can testify that I could not have been more wrong. The plans the Lord had for me were far better than the ones I had for myself. I continue to be amazed at the truth of Jeremiah 29:11 which confirms that God's plans are not to harm us but to prosper us. The Bible also tells us that the Lord will fulfill our destiny if we delight and trust in Him (Psalm 37:4-5). Indeed we can trust and obey God with all of our heart, soul and mind and follow Him one step at a time and we will never regret it. I firmly believe the Lord knows us far better than we know ourselves and that He helps us become what we are created to be for His glory.

Another aspect of obeying God is to do what He commands us to do. As human beings we find certain things not to our liking. But there are things in life that need to be done, whether we like it or not. It is in those times that we need an extra push from the Lord to do what we need to do, even though we may not feel like doing it. When I struggle with certain things I would rather not do (but know in my heart I need to do them) I ask the Lord to help me do them for His sake. When I can remember that whatever I am doing, I am doing it not for myself but for the Lord (Colossians 3:17), I find added motivation and enthusiasm and I discover that the task at hand is not so bad after all. This creates added stability in my life.

Next comes the command to "love our neighbor as (we love) ourselves." The idea of self-love is controversial in Christian circles. Self-love implies self-centeredness, which the Bible frowns on. The Bible emphasizes the importance of self-denial but not self-hate. There is a difference between the two. Self-hate will drive a person into depression but self-denial will set a person free from self-centeredness. When we hate ourselves, we are putting ourselves down and we feel worthless. When we deny ourselves, we are stepping aside to let the Lord take control, which brings peace and joy. The Lord values us as human beings and so should we. We have no right to hate ourselves when the Lord loves us. In fact, the Bible assumes that we know how to love ourselves properly. In his letter to the Ephesians, the Apostle Paul talks about how we (as men) all know how to love and cherish ourselves and likewise we ought to love and cherish our wives (Ephesians 5:28-29). Spiritually mature persons can love and value others in the same way they love and value themselves.

Now we turn to the subject of loving our neighbor. Who is our neighbor? Our neighbor can be anyone with whom we happen to be involved at the moment. Our neighbor is not always an easy person to love. We cannot always choose who our neighbor will be. Jesus used the parable of the Good Samaritan to show us that our neighbor could be a very costly person to love. It can be costly to love a neighbor in terms of time, convenience, emotions and in some cases material resources, as shown in the story of the Good Samaritan (Luke 10:25-37). Our neighbor could be our spouse, child, friend, relative or a stranger who happens to come into our lives providentially. Loving our neighbor with agape love is always costly and it stretches us emotionally and spiritually.

What is agape love like? In the 13th chapter of I Corinthians, which is known as the love chapter, the Apostle Paul describes agape love in action. Agape love is characterized by tenderness and toughness; it is characterized by grace and truth, just as the Lord Jesus was known to be full of grace and truth. On the one hand, love is patient and kind and is full of grace, which is the tender side of agape love. But there is a tough side to agape love. "Love does not rejoice in the wrong but rejoices with the truth", which represents the tough side of agape love. Love forgives and "covers a multitude of sins" but we are also to "speak the truth in love." Agape love is balanced with tenderness and toughness. The Lord Jesus was well balanced between the two when He was here on earth as Jesus of Nazareth.

Tough love helps us set boundaries in our outlook, attitude and behavior. The father of the prodigal son did not beg, plead or try to manipulate his son not to go. He was willing to let him go and let him suffer the consequences of his own choices but he was also willing to take him back when he returned. He was able to practice both the tender and tough sides of agape love. It is refreshing to review the life of Jesus as it is recorded in the Gospels. He was "full of grace and truth" with a balanced combination of tenderness and toughness, from which we can learn. Even though Jesus was full of compassion, he set certain boundaries. He wept over the people of Jerusalem for their hard heartedness and blindness (Luke 19:41-44) but he did not allow himself to become a martyr (John 8:59; John 10:39). He told his disciples to go out and preach the good news but instructed them how not to be frustrated if people did not accept their message (Matthew 10:13-15; Mark 6:10-11). He accepted the limitations of the people who were unable to appreciate his message (Matthew 7:6). Jesus told Peter to forgive his brother who sinned against him seventy-times seven (Matthew 18:21-22) but also told his disciples to expel a sinning brother who refuses to repent (Matthew 18:15-17). When we follow the examples of Jesus, we will be able to stay within emotionally healthy boundaries by recognizing the limitations of people who are unable to accept the love of God. Agape love allows its intended recipient the freedom to choose to accept or reject it. The tough side of agape love keeps in check our human sentimentality and keeps us from emotionally burning out.

Deep compassion cannot be sustained unless it is girded with tough love.

It is not easy to balance the two sides of agape love. Some people tend toward tenderness and others lean toward toughness. Many Christians, including myself, tend toward tenderness perhaps because of the general image of Christianity being a religion of love, which implies tenderness. Some of us may tend toward one or the other because of our personality or life experiences. All of us need to ask the Holy Spirit to guide us to reach the right balance in each situation we face. Personally I have benefited from both tenderness and toughness shown to me by people I have encountered over the years. I believe all of us need both. When shown tenderness, we feel grateful and encouraged. When shown toughness, we feel pain, which in turn motivates us to grow. But when we are dealing with people, it is not always easy to know which side of love the person needs at the moment. If there is a basic rule of thumb, it would be to avoid extremes. This is especially true when dealing with children. I have seen lasting harm done to children when their parents were extreme in either direction. When parents are extremely lenient, the children may lack opportunities to develop character. On the other hand, when the parents are overly strict, the children may have serious difficulties working through their rebellion complex. When dealing with adults, there is less cause for concern because mistakes can be more easily corrected with adults. But there is always room for improvement when it comes to learning to balance the two sides of agape love.

It takes much practice to learn to love our neighbor with agape love. We become emotionally fatigued in the process. We need help from the Lord to be able to continue to love. It is not in our nature to love with agape love. We need constant reminder, encouragement and help from the Lord to be able to continue to love. Erich Fromm in his book *The Art of Loving* describes agape love, calls it "mature love" and concludes that it is "the rational answer to the problem of human existence" (4). However, he also admits that it is very difficult, if not impossible, to practice this kind of love. I believe the only person in history who was able to practice agape love perfectly was Jesus of Nazareth. If we are going to be able to practice agape love, we will need to be surrendered to Jesus moment by moment.

Love never ends. The father of the prodigal son never gave up on his son who went away against his wishes but he was ready to welcome him back when he returned (Luke 15:11-24). It would have been tempting for the father to write off his prodigal son as "dead" and decide to have nothing to do with him when he returned because he had caused so much pain and grief for him. But he was ready to take his son back and forgive him the moment he saw him in the distance. Such is agape love in action.

We live in a broken world and we are all affected by it in one way or another. All of us have been impacted by the brokenness of the human race. Some of us have been emotionally traumatized. Some are victims of severe traumas from neglect, abuse or violence. All of us interact with those who have been traumatized and are in need of healing. We can all be recipients and conduits of God's healing in this broken world. We can receive healing from the Lord for our own brokenness by letting Him love us with His amazing love. The Lord understands, accepts and forgives us. He knows all about us and there is nothing hidden from Him and He still loves us. There may even be some dark secrets that we cannot share with anyone. But the Lord still loves us. He loved us enough to send

His Son to die on the cross so that we can be forgiven and set free from the power and penalties of our sins. We can boldly experience God's amazing grace by simply accepting it with thanksgiving and continue to grow in our experience of His grace. As we continue to experience God's grace, we can begin to understand ourselves better by gaining insight into who we are and why we do what we do. As we continue to grow in our experience of God's grace, we will be able to better understand, accept and forgive ourselves. When we allow God to love us and learn to accept God's love by applying it to ourselves, we will gradually begin to change from the inside out.

It is human nature to assume that we must first change ourselves to become better human beings before we can be loved and accepted by God. This line of thinking can lead to a religious system which is based on self-efforts to save ourselves. None of us are perfect and we feel guilty. When we feel guilty, we blame ourselves and/or others in order to deal with the guilt which gnaws at us deep within. We expend so much energy blaming ourselves and/or others that we have little energy left to change ourselves and grow. The good news is that God already has declared us not guilty because Jesus paid for our guilt on our behalf. God, the Righteous Judge, has declared us not guilty and we no longer need to expend our energy to defend ourselves. We can now spend all of our energy to grow the way God would want us to grow. We are no longer condemned but are free to learn not to sin (John 8: 3-11). The more we experience God's love and forgiveness, the less defensive we can become. I am learning that the more I experience God's grace in my life, the less I need to defend myself. For example, I am learning to receive criticism from others with less defensiveness. It is becoming easier for me to say, "I stand corrected" and move on without becoming defensive. Likewise, the more I experience God's grace and forgiveness in my life, the less critical I become toward the imperfections I see in others. It is a liberating experience.

The more I come to understand, accept and forgive myself, the easier it is for me to understand, accept and forgive my neighbor. I realize I am essentially no different from my neighbor. We are all in the same boat with all of our human frailties, though some of us may be more severely damaged and broken than others. We can all be instruments of God's grace to one another. We will not be able to "save" anyone but when we can see another human being in need of God's grace just as much as we are, we are being an instrument of God's grace to that neighbor. A healing relationship is one characterized by grace and truth with lack of defensiveness and condemnation. It is based on honesty and empathy. It is an "I and Thou" relationship as described by Martin Buber in his book with the same title.

It is easier to talk about agape love than it is to practice it. We may fully agree that agape love is the answer we are all looking for but to be able to practice it consistently is another matter. How can we develop the ability to practice agape love? We can learn from the life of Jesus. Even though Jesus was the Son of God, He "learned obedience through the things he suffered" (Hebrews 5:8). After a challenging day of ministry, the Lord Jesus was known to withdraw to a quiet place to pray alone (Luke 5:15-16; Matthew 14:23). It is not difficult to imagine that in those quiet times with His heavenly Father, Jesus agonized and sought help from the Father, which enabled Him to develop agape love. After a busy day in the world, dealing with the challenges of life, we might want to retreat to our home to relax or do things that would get our mind off of our challenges. By doing so we may be relieved of our stress and get rejuvenated to get ready for the next day, but our ability to love with agape love will not be developed unless we commune with the Lord regularly. We need to spend time in silence in the presence of the Lord for extended periods of time to quietly sort through the challenges we are faced with and agonize over them with deep groaning. It is in those times of deep silence before the Lord that our ability to love with agape love is developed. Without it agape love would only remain an idea with limited impact on our lives, even though we may believe it is "the greatest thing in the world." But with practice over a period of time, our ability to love with agape love can be developed and refined as we learn from the mistakes we make in the process.

In his book *The Art of Loving* Erich Fromm concludes that love (agape love) is "the ultimate and real need in every human being" (5). He goes on to state that "a society that excludes the development of love must in the long run perish of its own contradiction with the basic necessities of human nature" (6). Further, he notes (and bemoans) that the practice of agape love is only an "exceptional-individual phenomenon" practiced only by a few exceptional individuals (7). I believe this is where Christians can make a difference. In the aftermath of the 2011 "triple" (earthquake, tsunami and nuclear) disasters in Japan, thousands of volunteers poured into the affected areas to provide physical and emotional care. It is interesting to note that the secular news media in Japan made a point of reporting that a disproportionally large number of the volunteers were Christians. We, as followers of Christ, are commanded to love as Christ loved. Many Christians from around the world responded to the call of Christ to engage in acts of love to provide care for the disaster victims and this did not go unnoticed by the world.

We sometimes hear the comment, "But I am not Jesus." Perhaps we make such a statement to justify our failure to love as Jesus loved. Indeed we are not Jesus. Jesus was the only person in history who practiced agape love perfectly. But we are expected to become *more like Jesus* as we grow spiritually. Few of us may be gifted enough to practice agape love as Mother Teresa did but all of us have a chance to practice agape in our own unique ways every day of our lives with help from the Lord. In so doing we can become the light and salt of the world and make a difference as followers of Christ. We can do this, not only in times of great needs such as in the aftermath of a wide-spread natural disaster, but in our ordinary everyday interactions with our neighbors whom the Lord brings our way. I believe the Lord can use for His glory every act of kindness, random or planned, that we engage in when it is motivated by agape love. I believe agape therapy can bring hope to this broken world which desperately yearns for true love which is so rare. Agape therapy can be practiced by every follower of Christ. It would still be an "individual phenomenon" (a choice made by each individual) but when it is multiplied by tens of thousands of the followers of Christ, it could deeply impact a society.

Chapter Five

Summing Up

Summary and Conclusion

All of us face challenges in life. Some of the challenges we face are so painful that we invariably ask, "Why is this happening to me?" Throughout human history people have grappled with this question and have come up with various answers. Those answers may give us some mental reprieve from our never-ceasing struggles but the question keeps coming back with every new challenge we face. The Bible promises the day in the future when there will be no more pain or sorrow when the Lord establishes "a new heaven and a new earth" (Revelation 21:1-4). But until then "bad things" will continue to happen. But we are not helpless. Jesus said, "In this world you will have trouble. But take heart, I have overcome the world" (John16:33b NIV). By following Biblical principles we will be able to overcome life's challenges. The Apostle Paul reminds us, "No temptation has overtaken you except such as is common to man; but God is faithful, who will not allow you to be tempted beyond what you are able, but with the temptation will also make a way of escape that you may be able to bear it" (I Corinthians 10:13 NKJV).

We have discussed some of the things we can do as Christians in order to deal with the painful things that happen in life. First, we have the word of God to guide and sustain us. By learning to shape the way we think according to the instructions given in the Bible we can learn to maneuver the treacherous channels of life's journey. Secondly, as we deepen our relationship with the Lord by spending unhurried quiet time with Him, we can receive comfort, insight, wisdom and healing with the help of the Holy Spirit. Thirdly, by cultivating deep relationships with a few fellow believers who are willing and able to become listening partners with us, we will be able to bear one another's burdens and complete our journey in this world with victory. The word, prayer and fellowship are the basics of the Christian life. We need to get back to the basics, only in a deeper way. We will probably never know in this life exactly why certain bad things happen to good people. However, by following Biblical principles, we will be able to grow spiritually and emotionally and accomplish God's purpose in our suffering. When we grow deeply in our relationship with the Lord by following the Biblical prescriptions, the endless ontological question "Why do bad things happen to good people?" can be replaced by a more practical question "How can we bring glory to God through all of life's challenges we face?"

Measuring Your Own Progress

Emotional maturity and spiritual maturity go hand in hand. Spiritual maturity is gained when we are shaped by the word of God in our thinking and behavior. When we become spiritually mature, emotional maturity follows. The spiritual and emotional growth process can be measured. The changes will become evident to ourselves when we grow. The changes will also be noticed by others as well. When we are growing, we will experience a change in the way we perceive and experience problems. When we are growing, the problems of living will be viewed as challenges to be overcome rather than evils to be cursed. With the current state of the art, it is not possible to precisely measure spiritual and emotional growth. However, it is possible to obtain broad measures of spiritual and emotional growth with the help of measurement tools.

The *Spiritual/Emotional Difficulty Inventory*, which is attached in the Appendix, can be used to measure such growth. This inventory consists of a set of statements related to one's emotional and spiritual maturity or lack of it. The statements were selected from the ones used by the late Dr. Raymond Cramer, a Christian psychologist, whom I met in my early years when I was beginning to be interested in the integration of psychology and theology. In his book *The Psychology of Jesus and Mental Health* Dr. Cramer used those statements to help his readers identify areas of emotional and spiritual difficulties. I have modified the format. First, for the sake of convenience, the number of statements has been reduced to 100. Secondly, each statement has been assigned to a five-point scale in order to measure the severity of the difficulty being experienced. When all of the scores are tallied, the total number could range from 0 to 400. I have used this inventory to measure my own progress over time (longitudinal data). I have also used it to measure differences among individuals experiencing varying degrees of difficulties in their lives (cross-sectional data). The results have consistently confirmed my clinical impressions. It is a crude measurement tool lacking rigorous scientific validity but a useful one for practical purposes.

The reader is encouraged to go over each statement carefully and honestly to identify the level of difficulty being experienced at the present time. The areas that show difficulties, as indicated by high scores, should be carefully noted. The statements that are rated as 3 or 4 should be prayerfully examined as to their cause during quiet time with the Lord. One might ask the Holy Spirit to bring healing to those areas of difficulty. We might also bring them up during a sharing time with our listening partners. If they should present serious difficulties to the point of interfering with our functioning, professional help should be considered. One might repeat taking the inventory at six to twelve months' intervals to see progress over time. (Five spaces are provided to record the score for each statement to allow comparisons between inventory times but it can be extended to as many times as is desired.) As we grow spiritually and emotionally over a period of time, the total score should decrease, though it would be unrealistic for anyone to reach the total score of "0" and stay there. In fact, the total score may go up or down, depending on what happens in our lives. When faced with painful and prolonged challenges, the total scores will go up but as we work through the painful challenges and manage to attain spiritual and emotional maturity with the Lord's help, the overall scores will go down again. Life's challenges are always painful but when we learn to overcome them with the Lord's help, we will be able to reap "the harvest of righteousness and peace" as a result of the training we receive from the Lord (Hebrews 12:11).

It is conceivable that when we achieve low difficulty scores, which would imply we are spiritually and emotionally growing, we would be less likely to ask "why?" when faced with life's challenges.* Instead, we would be more likely to say "why not!" and take on life's challenges with confidence in the

Lord's help. In my own life I have seen a gradual decrease in the overall difficulty scores and I no longer ask why bad things happen to me. Instead, I ask myself how I might be able to deal with each challenge that comes my way with the Lord's help. Instead of dreading it I almost welcome the challenge, though not without some fear and trembling. Years ago when my wife and I were members of Hollywood Presbyterian Church, our pastor, Dr. Lloyd Ogilvie, had a weekly television program entitled "Let God Love You." Frequently he would challenge his TV audience by saying, "Welcome problems as friends." For years I wondered if I would ever be able to get to the point when I could welcome my problems as friends. I am not there yet, but I am getting closer.

*No empirical data are available to support this idea. It would be interesting to find out if there is a correlation between the spiritual/emotional difficulty scores and the frequency, with which people ask the question, "Why do bad things happen to good people?" In the event such correlation is found to exist, we must be careful not to use it to create "spiritual competition" among people. This type of information should only be used privately to measure our own progress and not to compare ourselves with anyone else (Galatians 6:4-5).

Epilogue

When All Else Fails

Growing spiritually is a rewarding and fulfilling experience. When we are growing spiritually, every day can be an adventure with no dull moment. However, the Christian life is a marathon and not a sprint. Finishing the race is more important than how fast or how well we might do in the short run.

A person may be able to live the Christian life in one's own strength for a while, relying on one's natural abilities and talents. With determination and will power some of us may be able to live the Christian life for a considerable period of time, even for years. But the day will come when all human resources are depleted and we are "running on empty." The harder we try, the more impossible it becomes to live the Christian life. Discouraged and disillusioned, some walk away from the faith or become cynical but others find the secret of tapping into a deeper and distinctly Christian resource, the grace of God. The grace of God is the favor God showers on us when we do not deserve it nor have the strength to ask for it. It is not based on merit; it is based completely on the unfailing, one-sided and unconditional love of God.

The Christian life begins and ends with the grace of God. Everything else is perishable. All things eventually fade away, except the grace of God. The grace of God can reach down and lift up the most broken person and make him or her come alive again. There are no sins that the blood of Christ cannot cleanse. There are no scars that the Cross of Christ cannot heal. There are no broken lives that God cannot put back together, if we are willing to die to our pride and shame and let God minister to us with His amazing grace. In its purest form the grace of God sounds too good to be true. It completely defies human logic. It has been said that the Gospel of Jesus Christ sounds *scandalous* when it is truly understood for what it is.

Reading Maugham's autobiographical novel *Of Human Bondage* I came away with the impression that the one thing that was strikingly absent in Maugham's understanding and portrayal of the Christian faith was the grace of God. There was much emphasis on the importance of human efforts to live up to God's standards, which Philip, the main character in the novel (now as an adult) found impossible to maintain, ultimately resulting in his abandonment of the Christian faith. Alarmingly I find that many people who profess to be Christians seem to have a shaky understanding and experience of the grace of God. Some Christians live such burdened lives, feeling secretly condemned. Even though they profess to believe that Jesus died for their sins, they actually live as if Christ never died for them. Some of us live in a constant and subtle state of anxiety, perennially wondering if our performance would be good enough to qualify us for heaven.

Humanly speaking, we can never know what kind of performance would be good enough for heaven. The overly sensitive souls always wonder if they are good enough for heaven, while the self-righteous (and blind) ones, like the Pharisees of old, would presume no one else but them to be good enough to stand before God. What is good enough for

God? No one will ever know. But we can stop this endless guessing game. The Bible declares that nothing we do will ever be good enough to make us acceptable to God (Isaiah 64:6). But the good news is that Jesus Christ paid the penalty for all of our sins to make us acceptable in God's sight. All we need to do is believe it and appropriate it in our lives. There is nothing we can do to add to what God has already done. What a relief! No wonder Martin Luther reportedly leaped to his feet when he finally understood the Gospel, the Good News of Jesus Christ. We are told there is no such thing as a free lunch. All things in this world come with strings attached. There is only one free lunch in this world. It is the Good News of Jesus Christ. It is free because Jesus paid for it on our behalf.

What we need to do is to live the Gospel as if it is true. The trouble with many of us is that even though we believe it, we do not live as if it is true. We have a tendency to go back to living in the way of man and try to earn our salvation by our own efforts. This tendency comes from our old nature. Therefore, it is an age-old problem. Over 2000 years ago, the Apostle Paul asked the Christians in Galatia, "Are you so foolish? After beginning with the Spirit, are you now trying to attain your goal by human efforts? (Galatians 3:3 NIV). If Paul were here today, he would no doubt ask the same questions of us.

Every day many of us experience failures and disappointments in varying degrees. It is unrealistic to expect victories in endless succession in the Christian life. No one can stay on the mountain top at all times. We must all come down into the valley from time to time. It is when we are in the valley that we can appreciate the grace of God in a deeper way. I believe sometimes the Lord takes us down into a deep valley so that we might truly learn to depend on the grace of God alone and not on our own talents or accomplishments. Those who do not go through the "valley experiences" do not develop spiritual depth. Without spiritual depth we will not be able to handle the spiritual highs without falling into the snare of spiritual pride. We must beware of the temptation to rely on the spiritually high experiences to maintain our spiritual walk.

The prophet Elijah went through what appeared to be a case of spiritual blues after his great spiritual triumph on Mount Carmel (I Kings 18:16 – 19:9). The great victory on Mount Carmel was not accomplished by Elijah's own strength. It was the Lord's doing. Elijah was merely an instrument in the hand of the Lord who worked in Elijah to enable him to display tremendous boldness and courage. Miracles occurred and the Lord was glorified. But shortly afterwards fear overtook Elijah. He became afraid of Jezebel's threats and ran away to hide.

Spiritual elation is sometimes followed by emotional depression. From spiritual elation on Mount Carmel Elijah plunged into emotional depression and the Lord ministered to him through an angel when Elijah was sitting under a broom tree, feeling sorry for himself. Spiritual elation can be maintained only for so long before our emotional energy is exhausted, resulting in an experience of depression. It is so important for a servant of the Lord to remember that the solid rock we stand on is not the miracles, not the great spiritual victories, nor the great mountain-top experiences. The only thing we can stand on that cannot be taken away from us is the grace of God. Everything else is "sinking sand."

It is tempting to substitute the spiritual achievements or Christian service accomplishments for the grace of God. We know from the Scriptures that certain things are of value to the Lord. But it is futile to prejudge how worthy our individual achievements will be to the Lord. No one knows our deep and hidden motives but the Lord. We cannot know in advance whether our spiritual achievements will turn into crowns or be burned up like hay on the Day of Judgment (I Corinthians 3:10-15, II Corinthians 5:10). The only thing that will stand on the Day of Judgment, that we know for certain, is the blood of Christ that covers all of our sins, which is offered to us as a free gift by the grace of God. Without being firmly grounded in the grace of God, there is no way a Christian can enjoy a long and fruitful life with joy.

Finally, even spiritual maturity, the very topic of this book, cannot be substituted for the grace of God. I believe spiritual maturity can be attained through consistent spiritual surrender. I also believe that the new nature in Christ can become more dominant with the old nature becoming less influential in our lives. We can move from glory to glory in our spiritual journey toward Christ-likeness. As we continue to walk in the Spirit, the fruit of the Spirit (Galatians 5:22-23) will become more evident in our lives. However, there is no absolute guarantee of permanency of the outward manifestations of the new life in Christ.

For example, even the most mature saint of God could be reduced to a mere shell of the person he or she once was when the person is afflicted with severe brain atrophy from an illness such as the Alzheimer's disease. Such persons, in advanced stages of the disease, cannot even remember their own names, let alone who God is. But we can take heart because even when everything on earth is seemingly gone, including our memory of who we are, the grace of God is abundantly available to sustain us. Our names were already written in the Book of Life when we first believed. There is nothing in heaven or on earth that can take away the grace of God.

Appendix

Spiritual/Emotional Difficulty Inventory

Please read each statement carefully and honestly respond by assigning a number between 0 and 4 as it applies to you at the present time. Scoring should done be as follows:

Never true	0
Seldom true	1
Usually or probably true	2
Almost always true	3
Always or definitely true	4

Place the score for each statement in the space provided. There are five spaces provided for subsequent follow-up inventories at 6-12 months intervals but one may choose to repeat the exercise beyond five times to evaluate progress over a longer period of time. Statements scored with 3 or 4 should be prayerfully addressed as to possible cause and origin and healing should be sought appropriately, with professional help if necessary.

I feel guilty about almost everything I do. ___ ___ ___ ___ ___

It is hard for me to get over disappointments. ___ ___ ___ ___ ___

I become sad easily. ___ ___ ___ ___ ___

I like prestige and authority. ___ ___ ___ ___ ___

I can't stop condemning myself for past sins. ___ ___ ___ ___ ___

I am troubled over my lack of self-confidence. ___ ___ ___ ___ ___

I feel like saying I wish I had never been born. ___ ___ ___ ___ ___

I am too concerned about my health. ___ ___ ___ ___ ___

I have a tendency to feel dejected and gloomy. ___ ___ ___ ___ ___

My sleep is disturbed. ___ ___ ___ ___ ___

I get angry when people nag me. ___ ___ ___ ___ ___

I feel nervous and tense. ___ ___ ___ ___ ___

I panic easily. ___ ___ ___ ___ ___

I tend to say what I think regardless of the consequences. ___ ___ ___ ___ ___

It is difficult for me to express myself in public. ___ ___ ___ ___ ___

I have a feeling I need to be punished without knowing why. ___ ___ ___ ___ ___

My feelings are easily hurt. ___ ___ ___ ___ ___

I resent being told what to do. ___ ___ ___ ___ ___

I dislike those who disagree with me and I find ways to belittle them. ___ ___ ___ ___ ___

I have a tendency to worry more than the circumstances call for. ___ ___ ___ ___ ___

I act on the impulse and think later. ___ ___ ___ ___ ___

I have a tendency to blame others for my mistakes. ___ ___ ___ ___ ___

I am always pushing myself to do more than I should. ___ ___ ___ ___ ___

I find it hard to adjust to circumstances beyond my control. ___ ___ ___ ___ ___

I feel that no one really understands me. ___ ___ ___ ___ ___

I am bothered about a sense of something tragic about to happen. ___ ___ ___ ___ ___

I keep failing to live up to my ideals of being a Christian. ___ ___ ___ ___ ___

I have difficulty getting started in the morning; I feel better as the day wears on. ___ ___ ___ ___ ___

It is hard for me to mix with other people. ___ ___ ___ ___ ___

I don't seem to be able to love anyone but myself. ___ ___ ___ ___ ___

I would rather give orders than to take them. ___ ___ ___ ___ ___

I resent criticism. ___ ___ ___ ___ ___

I seem always to say the wrong thing. ___ ___ ___ ___ ___

I am fearful I do not make a good impression on people. ___ ___ ___ ___ ___

I find it difficult to get over bad news. ___ ___ ___ ___ ___

It is easy for me to yield to the urge to do the wrong thing. ___ ___ ___ ___ ___

I resent the fact that people take advantage of me. ___ ___ ___ ___ ___

I find it hard to make a decision, and having made it I keep wondering if it was the right decision. _______________

I argue a great deal. _______________

I am always looking out for myself first. _______________

I feel I am not as happy as other people are. _______________

I would rather limit my friends to a few rather than include many in my circle of friends. _______________

I have lost faith in prayer. _______________

I am too tactless in telling people what I think about them. _______________

I can't believe God would pardon my sins. _______________

I complain a great deal about my lot in life, making comparisons with others who I feel get the breaks I deserve. _______________

I lose my temper easily regardless of whether or not the situation warrants it. _______________

I feel I need to be right always. _______________

I am very exacting and hard to please. _______________

I feel tired without physical reason. _______________

I am depressed because of guilt feelings. _______________

I feel insecure about the future. _______________

I find it difficult to refuse anyone a request, no matter how unreasonable it may be. _______________

It is hard for me to sit down and do nothing. _______________

I make unreasonable demands on myself and others. ______

I find it difficult to give in even though I know I am wrong. ______

I complain when I can't have my own way. ______

I have so much pep and energy that I wear everyone else out with my constant activity. ______

I find life so troublesome that I wonder if it is worth it at all. ______

I take the consequences of my actions too seriously. ______

I feel guilty when I feel I have not done my best, even though others try to persuade me I have. ______

I am worried about my appearance.

I am never satisfied with what I accomplish. ______

I tend to plan to do more than I can in a reasonable amount of time. ______

I keep holding grudges even though the other person wants to make up. ______

I can't stick to a thing long enough to finish it. ______

I brood over the mistakes of the past. ______

I can't believe God loves me. ______

It disturbs me that I love and hate the members of my family at the same time. ______

I feel I should be able to accomplish more and do a better job of it. ______

I get a kick out of giving a person a verbal lashing. ______

I lose interest quickly. ______

It is difficult for me to forget painful experiences. ______

I feel down in the dumps and discouraged with myself. ______

I don't like to meet strangers. ______

I feel people expect too much of me. ______

I feel under strain. ______

I tend to exaggerate my problems. ______

I feel people do not like me. ______

When I am embarrassed my face and neck become red and I break out in perspiration. ______

I worry about my past mistakes. ______

I feel ill at ease in meeting people, not knowing what to say. ______

I feel lonely even in the midst of a crowd. ______

I want more attention than I receive from those closest to me. ______

I am very critical of the people I don't like. ______

I am bothered by thoughts of suicide. ______

I can't stand it to be ignored. ______

I don't like myself. ______

I become too involved with other people's problems. ______

I worry over possible misfortunes. ______

I am afraid I am losing my mind. ___ ___ ___ ___ ___

I cry easily. ___ ___ ___ ___ ___

I feel sorry for myself. ___ ___ ___ ___ ___

It makes me nervous to have to wait. ___ ___ ___ ___ ___

I feel people are talking about me behind my back. ___ ___ ___ ___ ___

I don't trust people. ___ ___ ___ ___ ___

I feel I must be good to merit the love of God. ___ ___ ___ ___ ___

I am troubled by feelings of jealousy. ___ ___ ___ ___ ___

When I am in a crowd, I feel people are laughing at me. ___ ___ ___ ___ ___

Total score (1st time) (2nd time) (3rd time) (4th time) (5th time)

______ ______ ______ ______ ______

Date __/__/__ __/__/__ __/__/__ __/__/__ __/__/__

Total Score	Difficulty Level
0 – 100	Low
101-200	medium
201-300	high medium
301-400	high

Recommended Readings

The Problem of Pain by C.S. Lewis
Where Is God When It Hurts? by Philip Yancey
When God Doesn't Make Sense by James Dobson
If God Cares, Why Do I Still Have Problems by Lloyd J. Ogilvie
Why Suffering? Finding Meaning and Comfort When Life Doesn't Make Sense by Ravi Zacharias & Vince Vitale

References:

(1) Martin, John E and Sihn, Eunbyang Pricilla. Motivational Interviewing: Applications to Christian Therapy and Church Ministry, *Journal of Psychology and Christianity*, 2009, Vol. 28, No.1, 71-77.

(2) Byrd, RC. Positive therapeutic effects of intercessory prayer in a coronary care unit population, *Southern Medical Journal*, 81 (7) 826-9, July 1988.

(3) Christensen, Andrew, Ph.D., & Jacobson, Neil S, Ph.D. *Reconcilable Differences,* Guilford Press, 2000.

(4) Fromm, Eric. *The Art of Loving*, Harper and Brothers, 1956.

(5) Ibid. pp. 132-133.

(6) Ibid.

(7) Ibid.

About the Author

Ken Yabuki, a former pastor, is a counselor with Asian American Christian Counseling Service (AACCS). A graduate of Waseda University, Japan, he received his M.Div. degree from Fuller Theological Seminary and an M.A. in Psychology from California State University, Los Angeles. He has been active in the field of mental health counseling for over 40 years. He has also conducted "listening workshops" for Christian groups in Japan and the US. For further information, e-mail kenyabuki@yahoo.com

Printed in the United States
By Bookmasters